Nikkei Journey

Japanese Canadians in Southern Alberta

N. Rochelle Yamagishi

Preface by Ron Ulrich

Nikkei Cultural Society of Lethbridge and Area
Sir Alexander Galt Museum and Archives

Note for Librarians: A cataloguing record for this book is available from Library and Archives Canada at www.collectionscanada.ca/amicus/index-e.html
ISBN 1-4120-5935-6

Printed in Victoria, BC, Canada. Printed on paper with minimum 30% recycled fibre. Trafford's print shop runs on "green energy" from solar, wind and other environmentally-friendly power sources.

TRAFFORD

Offices in Canada, USA, Ireland and UK
This book was published *on-demand* in cooperation with Trafford Publishing. On-demand publishing is a unique process and service of making a book available for retail sale to the public taking advantage of on-demand manufacturing and Internet marketing. On-demand publishing includes promotions, retail sales, manufacturing, order fulfilment, accounting and collecting royalties on behalf of the author.

Book sales for North America and international:
Trafford Publishing, 6E–2333 Government St.,
Victoria, BC V8T 4P4 CANADA
phone 250 383 6864 (toll-free 1 888 232 4444)
fax 250 383 6804; email to orders@trafford.com
Book sales in Europe:
Trafford Publishing (UK) Ltd., Enterprise House, Wistaston Road Business Centre,
Wistaston Road, Crewe, Cheshire CW2 7RP UNITED KINGDOM
phone 01270 251 396 (local rate 0845 230 9601)
facsimile 01270 254 983; orders.uk@trafford.com
Order online at:
trafford.com/05-0836

10 9 8 7 6 5 4

Cover: The cover was designed by Rochelle Yamagishi, using photos by Karyn Yamagishi (of the high level train bridge in Lethbridge, AB--the highest and longest of its kind in the world--that evacuees crossed over when entering this city.) In addition, the photo collage was compiled by Brad Brown, exhibit designer, of the Sir Alexander Galt Museum in Lethbridge, AB (consisting of file photos from the archives).

ACKNOWLEDGEMENTS

Firstly, I must thank the members of the Education Committee of the Nikkei Cultural Society of Lethbridge and Area (Lethbridge, AB), for their foresight and support of this book project. The members of the Education Committee were: Pastor George Takashima (chair), Mac Nishiyama, Reyko Nishiyama, David Tanaka, Toshiko Tanaka, and Lloyd Yamagishi.

In addition, I must give credit to Ron Ulrich, the Executive Director of the Sir Alexander Galt Museum and Archives. Together, Ron and the Education Committee members had the vision for this book.

I had worked as a volunteer Guest Curator for the museum exhibit, "Nikkei Tapestry: The Story of Japanese Canadians in Southern Alberta," that ran at the Galt Museum in 2003, and was later asked to author a book to follow-up the success of the exhibit.

I must particularly acknowledge Ron's compassion for the Japanese Canadian people and his suggestion for me to write about "what it was like" for them. Later, in conversation with my husband, Lloyd Yamagishi, we created the idea to present the stories in novel form.

I am also deeply indebted to those members of my family and friends who were willing to share their memories with me and allow me to interweave them for the characters in this book. It is not characteristic of Japanese people to share their feelings and so I have been most appreciative of those who have allowed me to dig into their past.

In particular, I must thank the following for their contributions of stories, pictures, and/or vetting the manuscript: Morris Higa, Taka Kinjo, Victor Kitagawa, Thomas Nakashima, Reyko Nishiyama, Yoshio Frank Sato, Sir Alexander Galt Museum and Archives, Toshiko Tanaka, Masayuki Terakita, Karyn Yamagishi, Lloyd Yamagishi, and Teruko Yoshihara.

It is my hope that Japanese Canadians of all generations and experiences will see something of themselves, their friends or their loved ones in these pages.

Lastly, I am extremely thankful for the support of my husband, and children, for their contributions and suggestions, as I have taken the time out of my daily activities to do the research and writing for this book.

N.R.Y.

CONTENTS

Preface

Introduction

Chapters

1 Issei Pioneer – *Koshiro Shimazaki*

2 Picture Bride – *Hiro Komatsu*

3 Nisei Pioneer – *Ruth Uino (Shimazaki) Akagawa*

4 Issei Evacuee - *Yasutaro Akagawa*

5 Nisei Evacuee - *Tadashi Akagawa*

6 Sansei - *Valerie M. (Akagawa) Takahashi*

7 Yonsei - *Mackenzie Takahashi*

8 Hapa - *Robert Toyama*

9 New Immigrant - *Matsuke Kuno*

10 Redress - *Saburo Morita*

Photographs

Bibliography

Preface

Southern Alberta is a very unique part of Canada. It has long been home to the Blackfoot people. It was here that the North West Mounted Police established their first post to bring law and order to the rugged Canadian West and pave the way for settlement. It is a region that opened up with the advent of coal mining and agriculture in the early 1880s. These industries attracted settlers from western and eastern Europe, Asia, the United States, and other parts of Canada, all eager to make better lives for themselves and for their families. My own family came to southern Alberta in the early 1900s, and this region is a place I am proud to call home.

Until I took the position of Executive Director of the Galt Museum in Lethbridge, the history and heritage of Japanese Canadians was largely unknown to me. It was not until I worked with a small group of volunteers from the Nikkei Cultural Society in Lethbridge, led by Dr. Rochelle Yamagishi, as Guest Curator, to develop an exhibit called *Nikkei Tapestry: The Story of Japanese*

Canadians, that I began to grasp the role Japanese Canadians played in southern Alberta. The Galt's relationship with the Nikkei Cultural Society continues to grow, as the two organizations find ways to tell the story of Japanese Canadians in southern Alberta. This book is an offshoot of this wonderful relationship.

Nikkei Journey illustrates the story of four generations of Japanese Canadians in southern Alberta: the *Issei, Nisei, Sansei,* and *Yonsei.* These different generations have experienced unique difficulties and triumphs in settling this region. Each generation shares its own distinct story of how they have balanced their own culture and heritage and assimilated into Western society. It also tells the story of the *Idosha,* those Japanese Canadians who were uprooted from their homes on the west coast of Canada in 1942 and evacuated to work in the beet fields of southern Alberta. The *Idosha* were mostly from the *Issei* and *Nisei* generations of Japanese Canadians.

It is helpful to understand the historical context of the stories shared in this book:

Issei

The *Issei* were immigrants from Japan or Japanese settlers of Hawaii. Most *Issei* were from the landowning peasant class of Japan. They had grown up in the rapidly modernizing *Meiji* period (1868 - 1912) when Japan was emerging as an industrialized world power, and had come to Canada before the First World War. About 3,650 were nationalized in Canada before 1923. After 1923, Canadian nationality was very difficult for the Japanese to obtain. By 1941, the *Issei* had spent an average of 30 years working in Canada in fishing, farming and agriculture, or building up small businesses. Yet they found it difficult to assimilate into Canadian society because of racial differences. As a result, the *Issei* created a way of life in Canada that was similar to life found in *Meiji* Japan.

Attracted to the open agricultural land, the *Issei* were important participants in the early development of southern Alberta. By 1901, over 30 Japanese and Chinese were living in Lethbridge. More followed. Many of the early Japanese pioneers in southern Alberta settled around the communities of Raymond and Hardieville. The promise to *"hana wo sakasete kaitekoi"* (come home in glory) was a strong motivating factor for Japanese Canadians to succeed. Japanese immigrants became quickly known for being hard workers.

The Japanese who first came to Canada were mostly young, energetic, adventurous men with ambitious hopes. They initially settled along the coast of British Columbia. Some found the conditions too harsh and moved to Alberta. Alberta offered no better opportunities for quick wealth. Taking what work was available, they sought to make a success of themselves so that they might fulfill their promise to their families in Japan. It was common for *Issei* in southern Alberta to make a living as sugar beet farmers, railroad labourers, coal miners, cooks and domestics. Only a few had the means to enter into business.

Many early Japanese pioneers in southern Alberta were successful at this work and were able to make frequent trips back to Japan "in glory." Others, feeling that they did not achieve "glory," could not return and face their families. To "have glory" would mean amassing wealth, or achieving success through education or any worthy accomplishment.

Idosha

With the advent of World War II, many Japanese Canadians were uprooted and put in detention camps for the duration of the war The Canadian government felt that Japanese Canadians posed a security threat to Canada's war efforts and evacuated over 21,000 Japanese Canadians from a 100-mile long strip of land along the west coast of British Columbia. Many men went to work in lumber camps like the ones in Slave Lake, Rocky Mountain House, or Fort Macleod. Over 2,500 Japanese Canadians were evacuated to the sugar beet farms in southern Alberta in 1942. By the first week of June, approximately 2,250 Japanese Canadians, or about 370 families, had arrived. They were sent to work on beet farms in areas around Picture Butte, Coalhurst, Diamond City, Coaldale, Raymond, Taber, Vauxhall, Magrath, and other small towns and villages. By 1945, evacuees constituted 65 percent of the beet labour and were therefore an almost indispensable work force in the province.

The Japanese were docile and cooperative during the evacuation because of cultural norms emphasizing duty and obligation, conformity and obedience. Such cultural beliefs as, "*Shikata-ga-nai,*" meaning, "it can't be helped," and, "*Gaman,*" meaning "patience and perseverance," helped Japanese Canadians as a group to ultimately survive the events of the evacuation. The Japanese thought they were showing their loyalty to Canada by accepting the evacuation and cooperating with authorities.

On September 22, 1988, the Federal Government announced that the government would issue a formal apology and monetary compensation of $21,000 to eligible individuals of Japanese Canadian descent, born prior to March 31, 1949. A lump sum of $12 million would also be given to the National Association to administer and allocate appropriately, amongst its member chapters, groups and individuals. It was felt by a local committee of Japanese Canadians, that were lobbying the Canadian government for redress compensation, that a portion of funds received should be redirected back to the community. Japanese Canadians in southern Alberta helped fund hospital beds at the Lethbridge Regional Hospital, and provided a trust fund to a number of regional hospitals. The University of Lethbridge and the Lethbridge Community College were recipients of an Endowment Fund that provides annual scholarships.

Nisei

Canadian-born and Canadian-educated, the *Nisei* were a transitional generation that straddled two cultures. They were taught by their elders to obey the laws and be good Canadian citizens. To be accepted in Canadian society, they had to assimilate into the Anglo-Canadian culture. The *Nisei* learned their lessons well. By 1941, their main criticism of the *Issei* was that the *Issei* were "too Japanese."

Most *Nisei* were only children and adolescents during the evacuation. They felt humiliated by the evacuation and responded with silence. It was a subject that was not discussed.

The *Nisei* grew into adulthood just as full civic rights were extended to people of Japanese ancestry in 1951. It opened the door for this generation to develop a wholly Canadian identity for themselves. They adopted mainstream fashion, ate Western foods, and spoke Japanese only when required. Traditional Japanese customs and traditions were mostly set aside. However, in dealing with their parents, the *Nisei* still were required to have knowledge of, and respect for, traditional ways.

During the evacuation, many *Nisei* had to forgo a high school education; the Alberta government provided free access to an education for Japanese Canadian evacuees only to grade eight. After the restrictions were lifted, Japanese Canadians could once again purchase property. As a result, a number of *Nisei* bought farms to grow potatoes, beets, and corn, and to raise livestock.

When the *Nisei* were allowed to move into communities such as Lethbridge in 1951, they sought to work in trades, such as carpentry, gardening or painting. Others worked as labourers, at companies like the Broder Canning Company. *Nisei* also found work as domestics in hospitals and private homes. For those fortunate enough to have attended high school during the evacuation, they pursued higher education and entered into occupations such as nursing and school teaching. Other *Nisei* established businesses in southern Alberta, such as Bridge Brand Food Services, Jubilee Motors, Acme TV, and Tanaka's Greenhouse.

Sansei

The *Sansei* are the third generation, children of the *Nisei*, most of whom were raised in homes in which, except for food, there were few visible evidences of Japanese culture, and in which the events of World War II were rarely discussed by relatives and family.

Goals of achievement, interests and social values were engrained into the *Sansei* by their *Nisei* parents. They speak little or no Japanese. The *Sansei* often enter secure professions, and their upward mobility leads them into an almost exclusive level of social interaction with non-Japanese groups.

The pursuit of success is important to the *Sansei.* Most of the *Sansei* in southern Alberta have left the area in order to seek opportunities unavailable in the region. However, it is difficult for them to elude their fundamental connection to southern Alberta and the Japanese experience in Canada.

Along with the cultural emphasis on education, Japanese Canadians also see educational achievement as a means of improving one's social standing, social acceptance, and economic prosperity. Many of the *Sansei* were able to access post-secondary education through universities in Alberta and British Columbia. In particular, the Lethbridge Community College and University of Lethbridge created easier access locally in southern Alberta. However, for all the success that they have been able to enjoy, the *Sansei* have generally shied away from high profile positions within Canada in government or business.

Some *Sansei* have sought to reconnect with their Japanese heritage. Many others have sought even greater integration with North American culture than other generations of Japanese Canadians. For the *Sansei,* intermarriage with non-Japanese has become commonplace. They have moved away from the traditions and religions of their parents and grandparents and do not feel a strong need to intermingle with other Japanese.

For the *Sansei,* becoming educated and contributing to their wider communities are important emphases in their lives. The *Sansei* in southern Alberta enjoy a life different from their parents and grandparents. The ability to obtain post-secondary education has enabled this generation, like many others of the same generation of western Canadians, to secure professional jobs and higher standards of living. Their hard work has been rewarded with more acceptance and recognition than previously known by Japanese Canadians in southern Alberta. However, the *Sansei* who remain in southern Alberta feel a strong affinity for the area. As a result, they are active within their communities, working with a variety of community groups.

Yonsei

The fourth generation, children of *Sansei* parents, get further away from their cultural roots. In actuality, because of intermarriage, there are much fewer *Yonsei* than there are those of mixed race (*hapa*). However, both groups have their ethnicity "written upon their faces," and they are still subject to subtle forms of racism and exclusion.

Hapa

This is a new term for persons of mixed White and Japanese race. By the 1970s, intermarriage was more common among southern Alberta Japanese, due partly to assimilation, but also due to the fact of demographics, the lack of availability of Japanese marriage partners. In the 1960s, Japanese families accepted inevitable racial mixing, but their mixed-race children did face some difficulties as a result of their Japanese heritage.

I hope that you will enjoy this book as much as I have enjoyed getting to know the many wonderful members of the Nikkei Cultural Society. Thank you, Dr. Yamagishi, for continuing to enlighten us about the rich history and heritage of the Japanese Canadians who have made their homes in southern Alberta.

Ron Ulrich

Executive Director
Sir Alexander Galt Museum and Archives

INTRODUCTION

All the stories in this book are true, taken from books and conversations with people who have had these experiences. The stories have been put together to make composite characters, representing the generations or groups of people who make up the *Nikkei* group (people of Japanese Canadian descent) in Southern Alberta. Each story is told from the first-person perspective and reflects the style of speech that the person would use.

These are fictionalized first-person accounts, based on research and personal interviews, about actual experiences of immigrants and later generations of groups, including Redress work on behalf of Japanese Canadians. (All the names that have been used are fictional names. Any naming of an actual person has been strictly accidental and I apologize if I have named a real person, living or deceased.)

DEDICATION

This book is dedicated to my parents, Faith and Frank Sato, Niseis who were evacuated to sugar beet farms near Taber, Alberta. It is also dedicated to all the Nikkei who have connections to southern Alberta.

1

ISSEI PIONEER

Koshiro Shimazaki

I was born, Koshiro Shimazaki, in 1887 in a small village in Oshima-gun, Yamaguchi Prefecture, which is a big island off the mainland of Japan. We lived far away from any city, so people called us "hillbillies." I was a sickly child and when I was about four years old I nearly died from diphtheria. In those days, there was no doctor nearby, but my mother was desperate to save her second son, so she took me to a neighbouring village to a lady who used to help people with sickness. This lady told my mother to take me home, give me a bath and make me drink some bathwater. Somehow I became better and from then on, my mother did her best to keep me from harm and from infection.

Even though I had been a small child, I grew very tall, and as an adult, I had large hands and feet. I had to get my sandals specially made. I was sent to school and completed high school. In those days, hardly anyone went to high school, but my parents said that I should be educated because I would have to "use my brain and not my brawn," to make a living. Another problem came when the Russo-Japanese War started in 1905. My parents wanted to protect me and made plans to send me to Canada at age eighteen, so that I would not get conscripted.

Around that time, the village mayor had a friend who had come back from Raymond, Alberta. He was a Japanese businessman who was trying to get people to work on the railroads and farms in Canada. This man said that a wealthy man from Utah had built the Knight Sugar Factory in Raymond and he needed workers for the sugar beets. He warned us to be prepared for the bitter coldness of Canada and the terrible drinking water of Raymond. I thought I could endure what other people could. So it was settled that I would go to Canada.

I left with a hundred other men on the ship, *Mexico,* in January 1906 and we reached Victoria after three weeks. We stayed one night in Victoria and then moved on to Vancouver, where we disembarked and took the train for Alberta. The vast snow-covered prairies overwhelmed me. I had never seen so much land or so much snow. We transferred to another train in Calgary and arrived in Lethbridge, after crossing a high metal bridge. Then we went to Raymond by wagon.

When we arrived in Raymond, all of us men stopped at the McCarty Hotel boarding house where we were fed in shifts. We ate food that seemed very strange at the time, roast beef with mashed potatoes and homemade bread. Then we were divided into three groups and housed in three large tents, where we spent a very cold winter. I had been warned about the cold in the winter, but nobody mentioned the terrible heat in the summer. There were no trees to shade us and as we worked in the fields, the sun was almost unbearable as it beat down on us. But I gained valuable experience in farming methods and when the Raymond sugar factory closed at the beginning of World War I in 1914, we had the option of staying and working the land, or leaving to find something else to do. So I decided to strike out on my own in farming.

I couldn't borrow money from the bank because I had no collateral and no witness. But I was able to borrow some grain seeds from the local storekeeper, Mr. Green, with the understanding that I would return the seeds with my new crop. It took many long hours of hard work, and all done by hand, but somehow I was able to save a small amount of money and rent more land. Then one year, the price of grain went up and I was able to buy some land south of Raymond on the Milk River Ridge, where I grew mainly wheat, oats, and barley.

Some time later, I decided that it was time for me to have a wife and family to help with my new farm. I sent a letter back to my village in Japan to see if my parents could find anyone who would want to come to Canada to join me. In a few months, I got a letter back with a picture of the woman I was to marry. Hiro Komatsu was plain-looking, but she looked like she could be a hard worker, so I sent word back that we should be married and it became official when her name was entered into my family register in Japan.

Some months later in the springtime, I got word that I could pick up my new wife in Victoria, B.C. It was a long trip. I had to take a train from Lethbridge to Calgary, and from Calgary to Vancouver, and then take a ferry to Victoria. I had to wait six hours in Vancouver before getting the ferry. I was staying in the New World Hotel on Powell Street and there was a movie theatre on the same street. I had never been to a movie before, so I decided to use up my time at the movie house. I paid the admission and could not take my eyes off the screen. I had never seen moving pictures of people before.

When the show was over, I thought there was enough time, so I decided to stay longer and see it again. But when I finally came out of the dark theatre, it was past six o'clock and I found out that I had missed the time for the ferry. I had to wait for the next one, so I was late picking up my picture bride.

Hiro was the last one standing all alone on the dock, but she seemed happy to see me. She was dressed in a *kimono*, so the first thing we had to do was get her some Canadian clothes. We stayed overnight at the New World Hotel. We did some shopping at the dry goods store on Powell Street the next morning and then set out for Alberta by train. Because we were from the same village, we knew a lot of the same people and she was able to give me news of my family from home.

I saw the look on my new wife's face when we arrived at my farm near Raymond and I knew that we would need to build a house. All I had to offer was a tent in the empty field. But I had spent all my money to purchase this land and we had to wait a year before we could build a little house. We started raising grain and hay, and we grew potatoes, beets, carrots, cabbage, and vegetables, to sell for extra money. We were really poor in those days and we suffered. We had to work morning and night. There was no time off. We had enough rice to eat, but no green vegetables, just potatoes and onions every day.

I had to haul water in the wintertime from a spring down in the coulee. It was hard water, but we could drink it. I used the Japanese style from the old days. I tied two buckets on the ends of a sturdy pole and carried it across my shoulders. In the summertime, we would hook up horses to a sled and take the water barrels down the hill to the well and then the horses would bring them up. But in the wintertime, the horses couldn't make it up the steep slope. They would slip and slide. They just couldn't make it.

When the Depression hit in the 1930s, we had a terrible time. Everything went wrong. No rain fell all summer and the grain shrivelled up in the fields. Everybody was in debt. We were so poor. For years we couldn't afford to buy rice to feed the children. We felt so bad. Our only choice was to load up our wagon with some of the seed wheat and take it to Ellison's grain elevator in Raymond and ask the operators to grind it to flour. Still, there was barely enough flour to make bread and noodles for the winter.

A lot of Mormons lived in the area around Raymond. People in the Mormon Church were good to us. They invited us to their church activities. When they made Christmas cakes to sell at bazaars, my wife would get asked to bake too. One year, they gave our family everything they'd collected from the sale of the cakes. At the party after the bazaar, they put all the money from the baking into a bag and gave it to us as a Christmas present. Hiro started crying then and couldn't stop.

In the spring of 1939, we decided to move to a little house in Barnwell. There we could grow cabbages and other vegetables and I also worked as a sugar beet labourer. The three oldest, who were boys, lived that first summer in the farmer's granary. In the fall of the same year, we bought a larger house on the northeast edge of the town of Taber, adding a greenhouse and large cellar close by. The children went to school in town and helped with the farm work after school was over. With all of us working together, a few years later we were able to buy a thirty-five-acre farm and grow ten acres each of tomatoes, peas, and other vegetables. We harvested a good crop that year and things started to look good.

2

PICTURE BRIDE

Hiro Komatsu

I was born, Hiro Komatsu, in a little farming village in Oshima-gun, Yamaguchi Prefecture, which is a big island off the mainland of Japan. Most of the people grew things like rice and sweet potatoes, but just for themselves because there wasn't enough to sell. In those days, everybody ate mostly rice and vegetables, along with a few sardines caught by the fishermen in the district. Not very many people went from my village to work overseas, probably because we could get along quite well without going abroad.

We did hear stories about people living in the district of Inukami, on the east-central shores of Lake Biwa. This district was called the "East Lake Emigrant Villages," because so many people had had to move away. The great flood of 1896 was started by torrential rainfall that caused the level of the lake and rivers to swiftly rise and overflow. The entire village area became a lake and villagers were forced to abandon their homes.

Men had been leaving their families behind, to go as contract labourers to Hawaii in the previous ten years. This was the first contact that migrating villagers had had with a foreign country. Most families in the village had a father, husband, or brother who had emigrated to Hawaii, or later to Canada. They never intended to leave Japan permanently, but they were motivated by their dreams of making a fortune and returning wealthy to Japan. However, it almost never happened that way. Instead, they mostly worked as migrant labourers and sent for their families to join them in their new homes. But they did send money home, so it was hard not to think of Canada as a land of "easy riches."

My father quit the family farm and went into business as a shipping agent. In the old days, there were little wooden boats going back and forth between the island and the mainland. Later, there were larger steamboats and my father used to transport things like fertilizer or cigarettes. He wanted his children to have an education, even though people in those days thought that fourth grade schooling was enough, especially for girls. I went to primary school in the village until sixth grade and then my father arranged with a school teacher to set up a night school for four or five of us to get mathematics lessons on the abacus, reading, writing, and ethics, all done by the light of a coal lamp.

When I was growing up, most boys would learn a trade like carpentry, or go into the army. A girl would usually work as farmhouse help or do weaving, or maybe sewing, but for that you went to a sewing teacher. Everybody could see that there was not much future for them on the island, so they were desperate for a way to leave. Young women of seventeen or eighteen would make arrangements with employment agencies to work in the city of Matsuyama as maids. They would leave their villages and take the steamboats that my father ran. I overheard my father telling the girls not to be fooled by employment agencies and get sold to brothels. He had heard stories of parents going to look for a daughter, only to find that she had already been taken to a brothel. So I wasn't allowed to leave the island for the city.

I really wanted to go to America, even though at that time I didn't know much about geography and thought that America, England and Canada were all near to each other. My cousin had gone from Hawaii to Seattle in 1897. He used to send some money back to my uncle and aunt, and they were very proud of his success. Word got around that I wanted to go to America and one day an acquaintance of my mother's mentioned that she knew a man in Canada who wanted a wife. His father, Mr. Shimazaki, came to discuss marriage with my parents. I was only eighteen years old and didn't know what kind of man their son was, but it didn't matter to me. I just wanted to go to America.

My family was poor and had a lot of younger children to raise, so I thought that I could help out by working very hard, saving lots of money and returning to Japan. My future father-in-law said that his son, Koshiro, was doing well as a farmer in Canada, so I thought that I wouldn't have to do anything but housework. I didn't even think about the man or the marriage. Besides, I had never really thought that I would get married because I was so plain-looking and I had frizzy hair that was impossible to put into the upswept, pompadour styles that were popular in Japan in that day.

The marriage talks went ahead and I became engaged to Koshiro Shimazaki. I exchanged letters and photos with my future husband for about six months. I don't really remember anything of what we wrote about, but I got the impression that he was a kind man. But I thought it didn't really matter who I married, so I didn't care much about the details.

Both our parents approved of the arrangements and so I entered my husband's family register and moved in with my new in-laws. We held a mock marriage ceremony without my husband being present. We decorated the place with his photo and invited friends and relatives to the ceremony and to the small party afterward. I spent six months living with the Shimazaki family, just marking time until the big day when I would leave for Canada. My passport was issued and I left Japan in October 1916 on a small ship called the *Sadomaru.* My mother-in-law saw me off and gave me a beautiful *kimono.* I don't know how they could afford it, because they were really poor. I thought my new husband had sent money for my passage and other expenses. My in-laws were very nice and had encouraged me all they could.

The further the ship got from Japan's shores, the happier I became, thinking that I was moving away from a life of struggle and hardship. Unfortunately, I could not eat or walk for the first few days because of seasickness. They didn't have big ships in those days that could plough through the waves, so the boat was rocked to and fro in the huge waves. It was frightening and on the lower decks there were many disagreeable, oily smells. But by the last days of the voyage when the storms were over, I was able to enjoy the trip.

There were lots of other brides on the ship, all eager and looking forward to meeting their husbands for the first time. We had a lot of fun, laughing and talking about what our futures might hold. When we finally docked in Victoria after a two-week journey, we were all even more excited as we tried to pick out a familiar face from the large group of Japanese men standing on the dock. I remember one poor girl who refused to get off the ship. She was crying, saying that she didn't know her husband was such an old man. As for me, I was the last one left standing on the dock until my husband finally arrived. I found out later that he had gone to a movie and had stayed to watch it a second time, making him miss the ferry from Vancouver to Victoria to meet the ship. But it didn't really matter to me.

Koshiro seemed even more handsome than his picture. He was smiling a big smile and seemed very happy to see me. I wasn't especially happy or sad, but only thought, "Well, this is the man I married." My husband was a nice man and I had no complaints. We stayed at the New World Hotel on Powell Street for one night and the next day we went out and bought new Western style clothes for me, which I wore for travelling to his farm in southern Alberta.

I was surprised to find so many Japanese people on Powell Street, with many stores displaying goods imported from Japan. No wonder they called it "Little Tokyo." Any goods or services you needed could be found in the businesses on Powell Street. We bought a navy blue suit with a white blouse and necklace for me. I had a whole outfit, with a coat, a hat, and a pair of boots. That was the first time I'd worn anything like that. Back in Japan, I would see young women who worked before marriage as school teachers, nurses or telephone operators. I thought they looked very modern, wearing *hakama* (Japanese-style divided skirts), but I had never even had one.

We boarded a Canadian Pacific Railway train, travelled for a few days and nights, and arrived in

Calgary. During this trip, I had mixed feelings about this new country where I would be making my home. But I kept the anxiety hidden deep within me. The train travelled into the depths of huge mountains. On all sides there were snowy peaks and hidden valleys. There was so much snow and so many trees. Some of them were blackened by a recent forest fire, which made me more frightened of what would be at the end of the line. I wondered if there could be any village or town at the end of such mountains. My only comfort was to depend on my husband, who was leading me into the unknown.

From Calgary, we took another train, crossing a high bridge, to the town of Lethbridge and then a wagon trip to the village of Raymond, where my new husband had a farm. I came to Canada with a great dream. In Japan we had been told that Canada was a very rich country, full of wealthy people. I imagined a happy, peaceful and easy life. But when we arrived at the farm in Raymond, I was so shocked that I almost fainted. There was not even a house to live in, no electricity or running water. I was horrified to see a whole hog strung up on a beam. A neighbour had given it as a present for the bride. In Japan, the people who kill animals are called *eta*, or "untouchables." On my first day, when Koshiro cut off some ribs and cooked them and served me some, I could not bring myself to eat. I told him I wasn't hungry.

At first, we had to live in a tent in the farm field and sleep on an old, wretched wooden bed, something you would not see even among the poorest people in Japan. But there was no use crying. I had made the decision to come, and here I was.

As time went by, we got a shack to live in and then I had to learn to cook with a coal stove and to clean coal oil lamp chimneys. I had to wash clothes with a washboard, in hard water. The soapsuds turned into scum, like whey. I had to learn to "make do," with hardly any ingredients for cooking. It was a hard and lonely life. The closest neighbour was miles away and visiting could only be done with horse and buggy, and then only when Koshiro could take time off.

We struggled in those early years, but we had two children, which helped take my mind off my troubles. Everything was going pretty good until the year of the really bad blizzard. Our second son, Kozo, was only six months old and he had a really bad cough and high fever. The blizzard went on and on, and he just got sicker and sicker. We didn't know what to do. Koshiro said our horse couldn't make it through the deep snow, so we thought he should set out on foot to take the baby to the town doctor. We strapped the baby on my husband's back and Koshiro tried to find his way through the blinding snow. Somehow he got lost in the couple of miles to town that he had walked many times in clear weather, and by the time he made it to the doctor's house, our baby was dead.

When my parents in Japan heard about this, they thought that Canada was too dangerous a place for their oldest remaining grandchild. They got really worried and said that we should send our first son, Rintaro, back to Japan for safekeeping. An uncle and aunt raised him. We had three more children after that, two boys and a girl. Then we decided that we should send for our older son. When Rintaro came back to Canada in 1928, he was twelve years old and he didn't know us at all. He had to learn to speak English from the younger children in the family and I think he felt awkward and left out, but we were glad to have our family together.

3

NISEI PIONEER

Ruth Uino (Shimazaki) Akagawa

I was born near the town of Raymond, Alberta, where my parents were farmers. I attended public school with children of both European and Japanese origin and I felt like a "normal" Canadian child. We played schoolyard games of "Pom-Pom-Pull-Away," "Run, Sheep Run" and many others. I remember singing with native pride, "O Canada" and "The Maple Leaf Forever," for Canada was the country of my birth.

When I came home to my parents, except for their language, food, some items and trinkets, books or magazines from their homeland of Japan, they acted as any other "normal" Canadian parents would. Although they spoke Japanese at home, they encouraged me to read and write in English and adapt to the customs and traditions of the people around us. They shared the same values of honesty, hard work, respect for authority and a sense of fair play with other Canadians.

However, my mother being from Japan, and not involved much in the southern Alberta community, still held to a lot of the Japanese customs. She hardly ever went out, but was kept busy bringing up the children, cooking, cleaning the house, and feeding the chickens and pigs. As the youngest child, and the only girl in the family, my biggest mistake was being a girl. My next biggest mistake was being born a day before Girls' Day, March 3rd. If I had to have been a girl, why couldn't I have been born on this most important national holiday for girls in Japan? My mother never stopped reminding me of my "second-class status." At family meals, my mother served my father and brothers first, then herself, and me last. I always had to use the cracked plate and eat the egg with the broken yolk.

We had hardly anything to amuse ourselves with on the farm. My older brothers would hardly ever bother with their little sister, but one time my next older brother, Toshio, whom we later called Tosh, convinced me that you could taste fresh honey if you sucked on the hind end of a bee. He caught a bee, cut off its stinger and gave it to me. He laughed when I actually tried it and screwed up my face at the bitter taste!

When Japanese people had first arrived in the Raymond area, a group of men had formed a Japanese Society to carry on social and community activities. Once there were more Japanese families in the area, they purchased a building from the Mormon Church to start a Buddhist temple. In 1929, they sent for a minister for our small church congregation. I was only about five years old, but I still remember how excited we all were to meet the new minister and his wife at the temple on the day they arrived. People could hardly believe their eyes. The minister was dressed in a morning coat and his wife was in an evening dress. Never had such finery been seen in our small town! We found out later that he had had the morning coat especially tailored because someone in Japan had told him that a minister in Canada must have one. People had all hurried there straight from school or work. Many of the adults were dressed in overalls, with their faces tanned dark from working in the harvest fields. We felt lucky to have a spiritual leader from the mother country.

The minister held Japanese language classes at the district school in the summer while school was out. Some of the older girls went to pick him up, along with his wife, early in the morning. They drove a two-horse carriage over nine miles of road, and took them back afterwards to the temple where they lived. Even on the hottest days, he always wore a black summer suit that became white with road dust from the journey.

We travelled to school three miles on horseback, two or three children bareback on each horse. The front child would hold the reins. The others behind carried lard tins with our lunch in them and also carried the books at the same time. The Mammoth District School had stables for the horses, complete with hay for feeding them. After school on a hot day, we would return to our homes again on horseback, so tired that some of the younger children would be falling asleep on their horses. The lead horse would stop as soon as it reached the farm gate and then the child would awaken from slumber, get off the horse and open the gate so all could enter the homestead.

The schoolhouse was the lone building on the prairie. Our favourite teacher was a young, unmarried woman named Miss Mitchell, who taught grades one and two. She introduced us to a different world. My favourite author was Robert Louis Stevenson and I loved to memorize his simple poems:

I have a little shadow that goes in and out with me,
And what can be the use of him is more than I can see.
He is very, very like me from the heels up to the head;
And I see him jump before me, when I jump into my bed.[1]

My imaginary play world consisted of the carefree life of a middle-class English boy, far away from the dirt and dust of southern Alberta.

---

[1]Bock, Vera, illus., *A Child's Book of Poems* (New York: Peter Pauper, no date) 10.

I attended grades one to nine at the Mammoth District School. When I first arrived at school, I could not understand English very well. My older brothers had learned English at school, but we all spoke Japanese at home and there were not very many Japanese students at the school when they started. By the time I went to school, there were about twenty Japanese students. We only had about six or seven Japanese families living in the Raymond area.

I remember being scared to go to school because one of my older brothers had had an embarrassing incident on one of his first days at school. The teacher had explained an arithmetic question and then asked him, "Do you understand?" He did understand it, but he thought she was saying, "Do you want to stand?" which was something he definitely did not want to do. He shook his head vigorously, "No!" The teacher sighed, and to his surprise and wonder, she explained the whole thing again, while the other students looked on impatiently.

However, my experiences in my first two years at school were really wonderful, mostly due to my teacher, Miss Mitchell, who took a special interest in Japanese people. She was kind to everybody in the school, but she became my special mentor, even after she got married and moved to Lethbridge, where she continued to teach school. We remained close friends over the years and she retained an interest in Japan and everything Japanese. In her later years, she went on a trip to Japan and even took part in the ritual of public bathing. I was honoured to be asked to speak at her funeral when she passed away many years later.

I thought Miss Mitchell was as beautiful as a movie star, young and so full of energy. She would even take the time to visit our homes. I remember the day that she walked home with us after school to meet our parents. I was so proud to introduce her to my mother and they discovered that they were both interested in playing tennis. My mother had learned to play tennis in Japan and had set up something for a net near our house. Miss Mitchell and my mother played a short game before she left that day.

In grade three, however, a horrible thing happened at school. We had a different teacher, a young man from another town in southern Alberta. He was stern and not used to Japanese people. One day he caught some of us talking Japanese at recess and I think he was a little suspicious that we were speaking ill of him. Anyway, he lined up all the older students in the school, from smallest to biggest, grades three to nine, and made each one of us put out our hand to get the strap. It seemed like he just wanted to show who was boss. We all felt it was unfair and were shocked, but no one shed a tear. After that, some of the boys played some Halloween pranks on him. The irony was that many years later, I found out at a Mammoth School reunion that his son had later gone to Japan on a mission for their church and had brought back many items from Japan. This teacher then proudly displayed these artifacts in his home. He had come a long way from those early school days.

I was about fifteen when we moved to Barnwell, where I attended school until grade eleven. I got a job as a domestic with a farm family, the Jensens. There I learned a lot about cooking and housekeeping. At home, laundry day was a big chore and would last all day. We never had a sink, so we would put the water on the stove the day before in the wash boiler. In the winter, we had to melt snow. The next morning, we poured lye into the water as it heated, so the minerals and salts would come to the top as a scum to be skimmed off. The water would then be soft, so when the bar soap—P & G, Sunlight, or Fels Naptha—was rubbed on the clothes on the washboard, the dirt slipped off. For dishes, the soap would curdle into a scum with the hard water and stick to the dishes, so instead we would scrape the food off, stack them and pour boiling water over them in order to rinse and sterilize them. We were so happy when we got our first detergent. It was called Dreft and it worked better for washing both dishes and clothes. In the winter, we hung the clothes up to dry on strings strung across the kitchen, where they dried quickly from the coal heat. But in the summer, we hung them outside on the clothesline and they got such a wonderful smell from the fresh air.

The Jensens had a Maytag wringer washer with a one-cylinder motor—you could hear the "putt-putt" of the motor for miles away, but it was so amazing. It had a wringer, which wrung out the water from sheets and jeans almost dry. With five boys' jeans to wash and their entire winter fleece underwear, the washer was an indispensable piece of household equipment.

They liked the sheets starched. Making starch out of flour—we needed lots of starch for sheets and cotton dresses and shirts—was an extra chore. At first, there were lots of lumps in my starch, but I soon learned how to mix it into a smooth liquid. Then, the items would have to be ironed—what a job that was, with flat irons. I used one while the other two irons were heating on top of the stove.

The Jensens were a Mormon family and were very kind to me. I sometimes attended church with them and came to know about some of their beliefs, but then I started to chum with my second cousin and her friends, and we began attending the Knox United Church in Taber. Shortly afterward, we were all baptized as teenagers and we were given biblical names, like Faith, Grace, Lydia, Ruth and Esther. I took the name "Ruth," and was glad for the chance to get rid of my Japanese name, "Uino." It was hard for people to pronounce and I hated it. Other people with Japanese names often had their names shortened by the townspeople.

My oldest brother, Rintaro (the one who had lived in Japan), and my second cousin, Esther, decided to get married, although it was more or less decided by their parents. But I was pretty independent and big-boned for a Japanese girl, so I wasn't much interested in boys and it seemed like they weren't interested in me.

I would have wanted to go into teaching for a profession, but our family didn't have the money for higher education, so I went back to working on my parents' farm. I even drove a two-ton truck. In those days, in the early 1940s, there were no driving tests. My brother, Tosh, went into town and got my driver's licence for me at the registration office.

About that time, Tosh met a girl from a farm down the road. Mihoko Akagawa and her family had moved here from British Columbia in 1942. We were a bit wary at first of these strangers, because the townspeople lumped us together with them, even though we had lived in the area for years. The Second World War had brought with it a lot of bad feelings against the Japanese everywhere in Canada. Even though Japanese people living on the west coast of Canada were generally hard-working and law-abiding people, when Japan bombed Pearl Harbor in 1941, the government forced them to move inland.

Tosh had got some work doing sugar beets on the newcomers' farm and he fell in love with Mihoko. People called her "Mimi." In those days, we weren't allowed to go out on a date just one couple at a time, so Mimi's older brother, Tadashi, and myself would double-date with them. Eventually, I got to know "Tad" pretty well and we decided to get married ourselves first, within a few months. The Akagawa family did not have a mother and so I was to take over the responsibility of running the household.

This family had come from a place in Japan that used a higher form of Japanese, so it was almost like learning the Japanese language all over again. I had to learn "proper" Japanese cooking too, since my own mother had not been a very good cook. My father had been quite happy to eat anything that she cooked and never criticized her cooking, so she never bothered to improve. I knew more about English-style cooking from the Jensens and so had to adjust my thinking and get used to making Japanese food more often.

We got married on January 31, 1947, on one of the coldest days of the year. It was nearly forty degrees below zero Fahrenheit. It was so cold that one brother-in-law, Akira, had to stay behind at the community hall to keep the fire going during the ceremony, so things would not freeze up. My husband's family was Buddhist, so we got married in the Buddhist church at Dogtown, near Barnwell. My second cousin, Lydia, was my bridesmaid and my husband's brother, Jutaro, was best man.

After a month-long honeymoon in Vancouver, staying with friends of the family, I moved into the Akagawa house with my husband, father-in-law, and Jutaro, who was still attending high school in Taber. Tosh and Mimi got married a few months later. Tosh didn't like farm work, so they moved to Ontario for him to find work in a factory.

Within a year, we had our first baby. I remember that I did not show my pregnancy very much and when my time came, Tad took me to the Taber General Hospital. The nurse asked me why I had come. I replied, "To have a baby." She looked at me skeptically. The baby was pretty small, not quite five pounds. In those days, they insisted that you not get out of bed for ten days after the baby was born, so when you finally did get up, you were weak from not using your leg muscles and they put you back to bed for another couple of days. I met a special nurse there, who helped me with the birth of my first three children who were born in

Taber. Helen had no children of her own, so she took a special interest in our family and we remained friends for many years.

Our first baby was a girl. We gave her an English name for a first name, and a Japanese one for her middle name. Valerie Mariko was so small that we used an apple crate for her crib. One winter day, I bundled her up tightly in blankets and Tad put her on the seat of the truck while it was warming up. When I got in, I found out that he had put her upside down! However, she survived it and she turned out all right after all.

When our first two children were born—girls—the hospital called my husband in the middle of the night to let him know and both times he went back to bed. But when our third child was born, Tad got dressed and rushed down to the hospital to see his baby boy. Oh, what a sight to see! It had been a long labour because of a breech birth and he was a "blue baby." I was so weak that I couldn't even nurse him. I had to feed him diluted Carnation evaporated milk and he became very chubby.

We didn't have much of a social life, except for visiting friends and relatives. We especially looked forward to going to visit my friend, Tamiko, in Raymond. She was a childhood friend of mine who had married and moved in with her husband and his parents, in the Japanese way. The family was one of the very few in the area to have a Japanese style bath. They were a pioneer family like mine and had built a *furo* or Japanese bath, instead of using a washtub for bathing. It was built with wood in a rectangular shape, big enough for an adult to sit, yet deep enough for the bather to immerse the body up to the neck. The bottom floor of the bath was made with tin, with a space underneath with a grate to build a fire to heat the water. Since there was no running water, it was hauled in buckets. There was a thick wooden platform floating on the water for the bather to sit on, to keep from sitting on the tin. Skill was needed to step on the platform so it would go down evenly into the water, or the bather would suddenly find the platform tipping and end up sitting on the hot tin. There was also a drain on the slatted floor outside the bath. The bathers thoroughly washed first, before entering the tub. Water was precious and this kept the bathwater clean so it could be reheated many times without becoming too dirty.

Tamiko's in-laws were also very strict followers of customs from the *Meiji* era in Japan. The father-in-law was the head of the house, so at mealtimes he was always served first—the first bowl of rice, the first cup of tea, etc. and so naturally, was the first to take a bath. Then it would be Tamiko's husband's turn, then her mother-in-law, and Tamiko would be last. It was understood that the last bather cleaned the bath platform, the outside and the lid before retiring. They used to bathe every night, even during the busy beet season—the hot water soothed their aching backs.

During the cold winter days in the later 1930s and early 40s, the *furo* was the centre of social life. Tamiko's in-laws would have a "bath party," inviting the minister, who only had a Western style bathtub, and other friends who did not have *furos*. They would have us stay a few days and we would look forward to the delicious meals that her mother-in-law made. Enticed by the Palmolive-scented steam wafting from the bathhouse, we took turns enjoying the hot bath every night, a treat indeed when the temperature dipped to below thirty degrees Fahrenheit. The men enjoyed their *sake* and the ladies sipped green tea with her mother-in-law's scrumptious sweets. The old farmhouse was a recycled granary. A pot-bellied coal heater heated it and kerosene lamps lighted the place. We slept on mattresses filled with straw. But we all—visitors and hosts—eagerly looked forward to the visits, for it was an opportunity to exchange stories in a familiar tongue and then to soak many times in the healing hot water.

4

ISSEI EVACUEE

Yasutaro Akagawa

I was born in a small village in the prefecture of Gumma-ken, about three miles from Shibukawa, Japan. I was the third son in a family of three boys and two girls. In those days it was customary for the oldest son to inherit the farm. My next older brother went as a *yoshi* to another family in Tokyo. This was a fairly common practice in Japan for people who did not have a son and heir, to take a son from another family to marry their daughter and take over the family name. I could have stayed on to help with our family's farm, but in the meantime, not really knowing what else to do, I joined the army at age eighteen and went to war in the Russo-Japanese War of 1904-05. I felt lucky to have made it home because one day near the end of the war, I was with my friend sitting on a rock, talking over what to do next. We decided to get up and move on and no sooner did we move, than a cannon shell hit the exact spot where we had been sitting. We could have been killed instantly.

From that day, I had a series of lucky incidents in my life. After returning home from the war, I decided that I didn't have much future on our small farm, so when I found out about contracts for workers in the rice fields of Texas, I thought that I could make some quick money and then come back to Japan and buy my own small farm. So a couple of years later, in the company of a boatload of energetic and enthusiastic young men, we docked in Seattle, where we all had to undergo a medical inspection. Myself and a number of others were not allowed to disembark because we had something wrong with our eyes, "red eyes" it was termed. I guess it was an eye infection.

The ship then sailed on to Victoria and to Vancouver, where I was able to land and begin my new life. I took a room in the New World Hotel on Powell Street. As I sat in my hotel room, I had a ball of string that was unwinding in my hands. I thought it showed how my life would unravel in this new land. I felt lucky to have this opportunity to start a new life in this beautiful country.

It was easy to find other Japanese people, all up and down Powell Street, who had been in Canada for a few years. From Main Street to Princess Avenue, Powell Street was filled with Japanese stores, rooming houses, bathhouses, a bank, two Chinese *chop suey* houses and a movie theatre. It was there that I found out about the "boss system." The boss met you at the ship, then took you to a rooming house to live until he found you some work in a mine or camp. Then he took you to the Japanese consul and you never had to talk to a white man. I was found a job as a houseboy with a well-to-do white couple in Vancouver. I thought this would solve the problem of a place to live and also help me to learn English.

I received five dollars a month plus room and board and I quickly learned how to do laundry, how to starch and iron shirts for the businessman who owned the house, how to shine shoes with spit and polish, and even how to cook Canadian food. But there was so much to learn and I soon found out that learning English was not an easy matter. One day, while in the basement washing clothes, the master of the house called me and said, "*Dena*." I was engrossed in my work and was shocked to hear this Japanese word, which is a very crude and rough way to say, "Get out and get lost." I had been trying very hard to do good work so I could not understand what I had done wrong to deserve this treatment. To my relief, I found out that it wasn't "*dena*" that he meant, but "dinner."

After three years of being a houseboy, I thought I could talk, read, and write the English language pretty well. I wanted to get an "office job" at Kelly Douglas Company, a food packaging wholesale company. But my English was not good enough, so I decided to go to school. They would not let me into Lord Robert School at English Bay, but at age twenty, I finally managed to be admitted to grade three at Dawson School in East Vancouver, an area where there were quite a few Japanese families at the time. Except for English, it wasn't hard being at the top of the class in all subjects, or being the tallest one in the class, because I was the only adult. In the evenings, I also took some English lessons at the different Japanese missions in the city—which were run by the Roman Catholics, the Anglicans, and the Methodists. To earn money, my friend and I worked as night janitors for forty-five dollars a month, divided equally between us. We also worked at a bowling alley, setting up pins for thirty cents an hour. It was not easy work.

About this time, I heard about a Japanese man who had come to Canada in 1906 and bought twenty acres of land up the coast in Haney, a town on the north side of the Fraser River, about sixty miles from Vancouver. He had started to grow strawberries and found that it was a profitable business. He wrote articles in the *The New Canadian,* a Japanese-English newspaper out of Vancouver that helped Japanese Canadians keep up with the news in their new community. We were urged to start farming. I saved up as much money as I could. I wanted to try my hand at farming, something that I knew about from Japan. But I needed to save more money and decided to start working in a sawmill and later at a logging camp. I earned a dollar and fifty cents a day, while a white logger got five dollars. The single men lived together in rooming houses and spent a lot of their money on drinking and gambling. I didn't like drinking or gambling and I knew this wasn't the life for me.

A friend had told me of a ditch-digging job in Summerland, so I went there in the spring. I worked in both Summerland and Kelowna, in the lush Okanagan valley, for a few years. I worked in the orchards during the summer and cut fuel wood during the winter for twenty cents per hour. I lived with a group of other men, either in a tent or a shack and we had to cook on our own. Since I had the most experience with cooking, I became the camp cook. Some of the time I worked at a sawmill, cutting logs for fifty cents an hour. That was the highest wage in those days. It was hard work, but you didn't need any experience.

After a while, I got tired of the camp life and my thoughts turned to a family. I decided to try to find a wife. All the marriages were arranged in those days and no one thought of marrying anyone besides a Japanese woman, but the Japanese girls were all back in Japan. So I went to a place on Powell Street where you could get dressed up in a suit and top hat and get your picture taken. I sent the picture on a postcard back to Japan to my relatives in my prefecture. My mother looked around our village and found a suitable young girl. She looked the girl over and found out about her background. There wasn't any money involved and the girl didn't have to be beautiful. She only had to work hard and have sons. I wanted a wife, but I also wanted sons who could help me on the farm.

I sent over the fare and after some months, my bride arrived by ship in Vancouver. Her name was Kiyomi Hyodo, and when I went to pick her up, I was surprised to see that she was so attractive. I liked her immediately and we seemed to get along fine from the start. We were married in a Buddhist ceremony. There were several couples and everything was arranged by the Japanese consul in Vancouver. We followed the advice in *The New Canadian* and moved to the Fraser Valley to work as strawberry pickers. Life was hard. We both worked hard. We used to go to work when there was still mist coming off the land and it reminded my wife of Japan.

When our first son, Tadashi, was born in 1918, I was overjoyed. A Japanese midwife came and spent about two weeks with us afterwards. She herself had been a picture bride and fit in well with our household. She helped wash diapers, cook, and do housework. We paid her twenty-five dollars for her services, which was the going rate, even though we would have liked to pay her more, but we didn't have any extra money. We even had to cut up my wife's beautiful *kimonos* that she had brought from Japan, in order to make diapers and baby clothes.

Then our first daughter, Midori, was born about two years later. Even with having the babies, my wife looked after me and worked in the fields with me. We managed to save up some money and two years later, in the spring, my dream of owning my own land came true in the form of a fifteen-acre parcel of land, bought for fifty dollars an acre. It was virgin land covered with bushes, willow trees, and large stumps from trees harvested in the early nineteenth century. The property was in the municipality of Surrey, in a common area called Kennedy, five miles from the city of New Westminster, twelve miles from Vancouver. It was two miles from the nearest store and one mile from our mailbox, where the mail was delivered. The farm was at the end of Kennedy Road, with no neighbours in sight—and not even a shack on the place. The only things that showed that anyone had ever been there before were the property pegs that designated my ownership.

Clearing the thick, tangled forest was a huge task, all done by hand and horsepower. To uproot big tree stumps, some as big as ten feet in diameter, we needed blasting powder and that was very dangerous. A bad accident occurred with one of my neighbours. He lit the dynamite stick to remove a big stump, but it did not explode in the expected time. When he went to see what was wrong, the dynamite exploded when he was only a foot away from the stump. He was killed instantly.

In those days, neighbours all helped each other, especially the Japanese people. We had a system of financial obligation, called *koden*. Each family gave a small sum of money to a bereaved family, to help lessen the hardship and financial burden in the event of a death, and also to show our support for each other.

I worked hard, toiling day and night, clearing the land by hand with a pick, but eventually I turned the piece of land into a productive strawberry farm. I also built a gable-end house measuring some 24′ x 30′, consisting of a bedroom, kitchen, pantry, dining room, and living room.

The house was built on stilts, with a full, aboveground basement. We didn't have backhoes and you couldn't dig down more than two or three feet without hitting hardpan. A few years later, our second daughter, Mihoko, was born. About that time, I built a lean-to over the well, which produced plenty of water for household use. At the other end of the house was a bathhouse, with a wooden bathtub. There was even indoor plumbing of a kind. When we pulled up our water out of the well with a bucket and pulley, I devised a way with a wooden trough to send the water out to the bathhouse, along the outside of the house. This was a great achievement in those days.

Every morning, my wife would take the children out into the field to weed the strawberries, pick them, or pack them, to get them ready for me to take into New Westminster to sell. I would take some to the canneries and some I would sell to stalls at the market by the river. Midori would quit school early each year to help harvest the berries. She was smart enough to catch up on her studies at the beginning of the next school year.

At the end of the season, we would go over to a neighbour's, a white man, and pick his raspberries. When those were finished, we would get picked up by a truck that used to come around and take us to Sardis to pick hops. My wife took care of the chickens and goats for us to sell eggs and milk for extra money. We didn't drink much milk. We mostly had rice, fish and fresh vegetables, and some eggs from the chickens and ducks.

The last child in our family, another son whom we named Jutaro, was born five years later and shortly after that, we sponsored my wife's nephew from Japan, to work for us for three years to earn his independence as a landed immigrant. When he arrived on the farm, he didn't recognize my wife as she walked toward him from working in the fields, because she looked so old. Her face was tanned and weather-beaten, and she was wearing my old shirt and pants.

My wife was a great help to me. She got up every morning at six. She would be the first one up and the last one to go to bed. In the evening, she would be sewing or washing, or salting vegetables in the Japanese way. I was very lucky to have such a wonderful wife, who would work so hard with me and my family, to make the farm a success. Until the war broke out, we lived a good life on the farm. Then my luck ran out. In quick succession, my wife took sick and then we had to leave our farm and move to Alberta.

5

NISEI EVACUEE

Tadashi Akagawa

I was born in 1918, in the municipality of Surrey, which is now a suburb of Greater Vancouver. My parents were so happy to have a son, since it is so important in Japanese tradition, but also to help out on their farm. Shortly after my birth, all three of us caught the 1918 after-war flu, so myself, my mother and father all had to stay in the hospital for a few days. One of my first memories is walking two miles all by myself at the age of four—a third of the way through a trail in the bush, and the rest of the way down the road—to the home of family friends, to get a midwife for my mother at home. I had travelled this path many times with my parents before, but this was the first time on my own. I was the only one available to go and get help for her to give birth to my second youngest sister, Mihoko. In those days, Japanese women didn't go to the hospital, but gave birth at home with help from other Japanese women who acted as midwives. In a farming neighbourhood, there was usually one woman who was called upon, who had learned to help with childbirth. Since Japanese women could not speak much English, it was very comforting for them to have another Japanese woman to help out at a difficult time. This woman we called grandma, or *oba-a-chan*, since we had no grandmother in Canada. Her son was the truck driver for the Surrey Berry Growers' Association, so we got acquainted with the family and became really good friends.

Our farm was quite well-established by this time, thanks to the hard work of both my parents. We always had chickens, a dog, a cat, and later a horse, together with a couple of goats for milking. Our economic mainstay was to be strawberries, but we grew a lot of bush berries, like red and black currants, loganberries, blackberries, gooseberries, and summer and fall raspberries. We had a variety of vegetables and our homestead was surrounded with fruit trees, such as apples, pears, cherries, plums, and peaches.

In the fall of 1925, I started school at a one-room school taught by Mrs. Smith. Kennedy School went from grades one to eight and was a little over a mile from home on Scott Road. In those days, the winters were very severe. Sometimes it would snow two feet deep and then my father would put on his gumboots and break trail for me and my next younger sister, Midori. If it snowed more during the day, he would come to the school and help us get home. The first day of school in September, my father took me to the schoolhouse and introduced me to the teacher. After that, Tom and Anne McDonald, who were brother and sister, and lived down the road from us on Sandell Road, befriended me and took me to school each day.

My father had joined the Surrey Berry Growers' Association. On the strength of his earnings on a bumper crop one year, he took the whole family to Japan on a trip, the one and only time. The Association was shipping his berries through their outlet. By the summer of 1926, he had done so well in his strawberry production that he was named the "Strawberry King" of Surrey.

Things seemed to move at a faster pace from that point on. Father decided that he needed a better form of transportation, so he purchased a horse and a small two-seater buggy with a box on the back, called a "democrat." We had hoped that the horse would do some work on the farm to relieve the pressure. Unfortunately, things didn't work as well as we had planned them. The horse was a little too high-spirited to be attached to equipment such as a cultivator or a stone-boat, which was a heavy sled-type of equipment for transporting material around. When we took him on the road with the democrat, he would spook and go tearing down the road at high speed and we had a hard time slowing him down. We had to hang on for dear life. It's a wonder we didn't get killed.

One afternoon when the whole family was on an outing to visit friends, father slipped and fell between the wheel and the buggy, but fortunately we got the horse stopped before he was hurt too badly. We tried our best to get the horse accustomed to farm work, but gave it up after about a year and a few scary incidents. We eventually sold him and went back to renting a horse when we needed one for farm work. In later years, however, we were able to purchase a tamer horse that we were able to use for riding and farm work.

When we wanted to go to New Westminster or Vancouver, we walked past the school to a station to catch the Interban, a heavy "streetcar" that travelled from Vancouver to Chilliwack. It came by our Kennedy station at 8:45 a.m. and came back at 8:30 p.m., so it was quite handy for us, except for the walk to the station. However, when I was ten years old I had to have my tonsils removed at the hospital in New Westminster. My father took me on the back carrier of his bicycle about seven miles to the Royal Columbian Hospital in New Westminster and returned for me the next day. We didn't take the streetcar because it went right into the city, about one and a half miles from the hospital, and we would have had to take a taxi the rest of the way. That was quite a trip, but we both survived it. Two years later, he did it all over again, this time with my sister, Midori.

Things went pretty well on the farm with all the different types of fruit, and in 1928, my father decided that we needed a new house. A friend of the family, along with his brother, helped us and I was old enough to be able to help too. We built a two-storey building, 24′ x 30′ with a full five-foot open veranda, and on the main floor a living room with a fireplace, kitchen/dining room, storeroom, pantry, and master bedroom. From the kitchen there was a stairway to two bedrooms. We didn't have central heating, but we had a wood stove in the dining room adjoining the kitchen, where we spent many a cozy evening, reading and eating snacks before finally going to our cold beds.

My mother had a real "green thumb" when it came to growing flowers. She planted pink carnations all down one side of our one hundred fifty-foot driveway, from Kennedy Road to the house. They were quite a sight to see. She also grew beautiful red peonies, asters, and dahlias of mixed colours in front of the house.

About this time, my cousin came from Japan. We sponsored him to work for us for three years to earn his independence as a landed immigrant. The last child in our family had been born a short time earlier, a boy named Jutaro, and he was a little mischief-maker. Jutaro got into a lot of trouble while my cousin and I were trying to work around the farm. One day my little brother was being such a nuisance, that my cousin lost patience and tied Jutaro to a fencepost to keep him out of the way and out of trouble. Another time, my brother kept poking at a hornets' nest, even though I had told him, over and over again, to stop. He finally got the hornets so stirred up that they swarmed all over him. When he cried for help, I rushed to pick him up and get into the house. The hornets didn't even touch me. Somehow they knew who was the culprit!

My cousin and I dug a new well at the back of the new house and built a shed over it, extending the wall over the bathhouse or *ofuro-ba.* The *furo* was a wooden tub about 30″x 36″ with a heavy piece of tin on the bottom so you could burn a fire underneath to heat the water. It had a platform on the side so you could scrub yourself clean before you entered the tub to soak. There was a floating wooden rack to sit on while soaking. It was weighted down with rocks on the corners. It wasn't like a Canadian tub where you scrub in your own dirty water. When you went into this tub, you were already clean.

In 1929, we built a new woodshed beside the new house and built a garage onto it on one end, as father had bought an old Model-T truck that needed to be cranked to start it. It was a stubborn thing. We didn't know much about trucks and sometimes had to jack up the rear wheels and crank our hearts out. The road wasn't wide enough for my father and he wandered all over and finally into the ditch. I don't remember how many times we helped him out of dry or muddy ditches.

But he had only one really bad accident, going uphill near the top of Scott Hill. He tipped the truck upside down. Luckily, no one got seriously hurt. My father, mother, little brother, and cousin were in the front seat of the truck. When my mother heard Jutaro cry, she knew that he was OK.

Over the years, we tried our hand at raising chickens, for meat and eggs, then Angora rabbits for wool for the English market. All went well until the "Hungry Thirties" caught up to us. We saw it coming, so we cut down the rabbit numbers, but we still had a lot of rabbit meat to dispose of. We sold a lot, ate a lot of rabbit stew and canned a lot, but there is a limit to how much you can use. Unfortunately, we had to destroy a lot of the animals.

In 1932, we bought a newer Dodge truck, a big improvement over the old Model-T. With the standard gear shift and all, I became the boss of this new vehicle and father had to learn to drive all over again. A few years later, we sponsored my cousin's next younger brother. During the summer and fall of this period, we went out to the surrounding area to do odd jobs when work was slack on the farm. We went to Sardis to pick hops and we earned about a dollar a day. At the end of a hot day we often treated ourselves to a ten-cent bottle of pop and we got two cents back on the empties.

I was attending Cloverdale High School in my second year at the time that my father developed arthritis in his right arm and couldn't raise it any more. My mother, cousin, and I tried to carry on without him but it was getting impossible, so I had to quit school and take over the farm. As head of the family now, I decided to make some drastic changes and build a hothouse for rhubarb, which was very popular at the time. My father's ingenuity in building must have rubbed off along the way. Somehow he had learned about Canadian building styles because they didn't use nails in Japan. He had worked hard to get things going, but now that he had me to run the farm, he turned his mind to what he liked best.

My father had an intellectual mind and was a great organizer. He liked to be in charge of the proceedings, going to meetings and being in the middle of things. Along with two other entrepreneurs, he organized a new association called the Highland Berry Growers' Association. Then about two years later, he started the South Fraser Berry Growers' Association, which took in the areas to Fort Langley, Aldergrove, Whonnock, Sullivan, Strawberry Hill, Alderside, Portmann, Coquitlam, and a few other places. We sold our berries through our new outlet. They were big-time operators now. The Growers' Association negotiated with different wholesale outlets and different canneries and started their own $S0_2$ plant that sugar-froze our strawberries for later use. Through this process, the whole strawberries were covered with sugar and stored in barrels to make into jam later on. The whole enterprise was a thriving success.

Midori loved animals and took most of the responsibility for them on our farm, even though her old goat, Shirley, was a real rascal. One day Shirley got out of her pen and chased our mother to the well. Mother was afraid of her and was forced to climb up to the top of the well casing for safety. She was waving and calling to us out in the field to come and rescue her. Another time, Midori had just got the mail and was walking back to the house while reading a letter from an old friend. Shirley ran up to be petted, but my sister was engrossed in the letter, so Shirley grabbed the letter out of her hand and ate it before my sister could get it away. Midori never did get to read the letter. Another time, we found Shirley staggering around and we thought she was sick, but when we looked closer, we found that her mouth was all stained red and she reeked of alcohol. We discovered that she had helped herself to a pile of strawberries by the packing shed that had fermented in the hot weather. She had eaten them until she got drunk!

Around that time, the world of electricity came within our reach. It cost us extra to bring it up Kennedy Road from Sandell Road, but we went for it because it was progress! Wiring the house was the first priority. A friend helped us get started until I "learned the ropes." Once we had electric lights, we were lit up like a

Christmas tree for a few days. I went uptown and bought an old used radio for our mantel. It was wonderful to turn the knob and get the news and hear all the latest hits. Until that time, the house had been silent except for our wind-up gramophone. Now we had to buy the weekly *Hit Parade Magazine* to read about the songs we heard on the radio.

The electrical system was installed, so our next move was a water system. I proceeded to build a pump-house next to the well-house. I installed the new pump, pipe and fittings to funnel water into the house, the rhubarb hothouses, and bathhouse. I was quite proud of my efforts in getting the waterworks installed on the farm, with the help of an instruction book.

In the spring of 1938, we bought a brand, spanking new three-quarter-ton Chevrolet truck. I took the steel box off and installed a deck on it with a rack around it, for hauling strawberry crates. For the next three years, things prospered on the farm. We broke more virgin land, increased our strawberry and rhubarb acreage, and our production grew. We were employing up to about sixteen berry pickers at the peak of the season. We were having a great time with good crops, though I had to work very hard during the summer months. I went to bed at 1:00 a.m. and my mother and I were up at 6:00 a.m. to get all the workers on the field with their new assignments.

However, a couple of years later in the spring, disaster struck. Mother had never been one to complain, so by the time we took her to the doctor for stomach pains, she was diagnosed with incurable cancer. They said there was nothing they could do for her in the hospital. They thought she would be more comfortable dying at home, as long as Midori could administer her injections of pain medication. Mother suffered through our busy summer season and Midori lovingly nursed her throughout her illness. The farm was in turmoil, but we managed somehow. We had to hire a cook to feed the crew. It was a sad day on July 24, 1941, when she finally passed away. I had lost not only my mother, but also my business partner.

Midori then took sick after long hours of nursing mother. It took its toll after months of heavy lifting, of turning her over in bed, and in the last days, supporting mother's body with her outstretched arms underneath her, trying to prevent our mother's body from touching the bed. At that point our mother was just "skin and bones." When mother died, Midori had a "nervous breakdown" and couldn't talk or respond. She lost all her memory and couldn't even recognize us. The doctor wanted to put her in the hospital, but the family didn't want her to go in. Then a good friend of the family insisted on taking care of her. She took Midori to a chiropractor friend. We had to half carry and half drag her into the elevator, then up to the sixth floor, and to the office, to get a treatment on her neck. The chiropractor said that her head had "fallen off its axis." Two days later, we went for another treatment and she walked in on her own on the elevator and even the elevator operator was amazed.

From that point on, Midori improved, with the help of loving care and herbal tea. When she became well enough to travel, these friends took my sister and I on a trip up the Fraser Canyon, through Hope and Merritt to Kamloops and Tranquill. Thanks to our friends, Midori made a full recovery.

When Japan struck Pearl Harbor on December 7, 1941, we couldn't believe it. As a result of the attack, we were all called "enemy aliens" if we were of Japanese ancestry, regardless of being second-generation or naturalized Canadian citizens. Suddenly, we were a mass of people without a country. We were frozen. The B.C. Security Commission seized all our boats, cars, and trucks. At the beginning of February 1942, a poster signed by Louis St. Laurent, the Minister of Justice for Canada, gave notice to all people of Japanese racial origin that it was our duty to bring in our vehicles, cameras, firearms, ammunition and explosives, and radios, even our beloved mantel radio that we had enjoyed so much. Most of us lined up willingly to turn in our possessions. I asked the officer at the RCMP detachment, "Why radios?" He said that they could be made into short-wave senders. It seemed like the rest of the people in Canada thought we probably were all spies.

We couldn't make a move without permission. Immediately, the non-naturalized first-generation people were all sent to road camps to build highways. Most of these people had families and the expulsion order was just tearing the families apart. The men went to road camps under the guard of the RCMP and soldiers. The women, children, and grandmothers who didn't even speak English, were left behind. The work in the road camps was hard. They had no big machines like bulldozers. They had to just use their hands, with a pick, shovel or axe. It was all rock, gravel, and big, big trees. It was like prison.

All Japanese were on curfew. We had to be indoors after dark. We were to be moved a hundred miles from the coastline, either to the interior ghost towns of Kaslo, Sandon, Tappen, New Denver, Slocan, Greenwood, Grand Forks, and others, or to the sugar beet fields of Alberta or Manitoba. There was talk for a while that Canadian-born and naturalized Canadians would be able to stay in our homes, but we soon found out that that was not to be.

Life was confusion for the next five months until the government got all the paperwork in order. We were lucky to be able to stay on our individual farms until we were shipped out in April 1942, along with the ones who lived in the city. But the people from all the islands were herded into the animal stalls that weren't even cleaned, called Hastings Park, at the Vancouver Exhibition Grounds. They were cattle barns, big buildings with no heating. Bunk beds had been brought in and mothers would put up blankets to make little rooms so their families could have a little privacy, but the conditions were horrible.

We all bided our time during those five months, hoping that there might be some changes made in our distribution plans, but no such luck. The final axe fell on us in our district and it was time for us to go. On the morning of April 11, 1942, we were to be ready for the truck to pick us up. With just a couple of weeks notice, each of us was to have packed a hundred fifty pounds of our life's possessions.

We were led to believe that we would be allowed to return to our home and belongings as soon as the war was over, so we left our good china and packed our old. The baggage limit caused some difficult decisions. We left some "treasures" in the house, hoping to be back some day. We had a *samurai* sword of my father's, brought from Japan, which was left in the attic. They had never asked about swords, so we had forgotten to take it in.

My sister, Mihoko, managed to sneak in some of her favourite books and Jutaro smuggled in some of his records and the gramophone. We took our bicycle, our sewing machine, some dishes and cooking utensils, our bedding, some clothing, gardening and work tools, and lunch for the three-day journey.

Midori had planned to be married in January 1942. All the arrangements for a big wedding reception had been made, but were never to be carried out. The groom, Akira Yasuda, was a fisherman and the day after the Pearl Harbor attack, fishing vessels had started to be impounded. He was in Vancouver, helping with wedding plans, when he got word that he was required by the B.C. Securities Commission to motor his fishing boat from its usual docking site at Ucluelet, on the west coast of Vancouver Island, to New Westminster in the south. About twelve hundred fishing boats, which were owned or operated by naturalized citizens or *Nisei*, were impounded there. Because of the curfew, people couldn't stay out after dark to attend the wedding reception and we didn't really know what would happen when Akira took his boat, so we decided to move the wedding up, to just a week after Pearl Harbor. After a short afternoon wedding service in the United Church on Powell Street, the couple had beautiful studio pictures taken of a wedding that was never celebrated properly. Midori looked really lovely in a satin gown with a long train. Then the couple went home with family friends. But the next day, when my sister said good-bye to her new husband, she didn't really know whether she would ever see him again.

These were very uncertain times and the boat trip was dangerous. It was a long and unusual trip for the small fishing boats to make down the west coast of the Island in the open Pacific Ocean. A few years earlier, one of Akira's brothers had been capsized in the ocean on a routine trip. A number of boats had been travelling together, as was the custom, with the fishermen watching out for each other in the huge waves. Suddenly, Akira's brother's boat had disappeared from sight and when Akira went back to check, he found his brother clinging to a piece of wreckage in the cold water. The boat was never recovered. It had been a near miss.

When Akira did return from his boat trip, we managed to have a wedding dinner at the house in Surrey after the New Year, with just a few friends, but the groom's family was unable to attend because of the curfew. Until they received their evacuation orders, Midori and Akira went to live with his family in Steveston, one of the many villages on the coast where fish processing plants were located. Akira's father had worked as a fish packer. He would take his boat out to meet the fishermen, to buy fish from them and take their catch back to the cannery, so that they could continue with their fishing.

As we awaited the outcome of the government decision, as to who would have to move and when we would have to go, we did less and less work on our strawberry crop. I can still picture my father pacing before his acres of strawberries and fruit trees that were in full blossom. He must have felt bitter about the many years of hard labour about to be snatched away from him. We decided that it would be best to move to a sugar beet farm in southern Alberta, believing that remaining as a family unit would be less heartbreaking. It was a frantic time for us. We had some vegetables in the cellar, a horse, and some goats to sell, at whatever price we could get. The farm and the crops, ready to be harvested soon, would all be a complete loss. We ignored the curfew and ran around selling what we could. We literally ran around, as we had no truck. We had decided to give it away to family friends, rather than have it impounded and perhaps never returned.

We shed some tears, said good-bye to our home, our farm and our horse, Prince, hoping someone would look after him. We left him in the pasture with a big tub full of water and left the gate open, so that if no one came to his rescue, he could get out and fend for himself.

We had been notified that pick-up time for us would be eight o'clock in the morning. But the truck arrived much earlier. It distressed my sister greatly to have to leave the breakfast dishes unwashed and the coffee pot still on a hot stove. That was how we left the home of our childhood on the morning of April 11, 1942.

We left the New Westminster train station at 9:00 a.m. with all our white friends wishing us the best. I couldn't help wondering, "The best of what?" We really had no idea where we were going or what was in store for us. We were herded into an old CPR passenger train with wooden slatted seats, which was to be our home for the next three days. It was just a coach stuck on the end of a freight train.

I smuggled our pet dog, "Nellie," on the train without anyone seeing her tucked inside my jacket. She was Mihoko's dog and we knew she would be heart-broken if we left her. We were well into the Rockies when the conductor came by and noticed the dog. He was very displeased, but I explained that I couldn't leave her on the farm, so I had brought her. He must have had a dog at one time. He realized that we couldn't turn her loose in the mountains, so he said to be sure to let her out every time we stopped. We promised to keep her quiet. We had no more trouble after he noticed how good the dog was and he even petted her when he went by. She was pregnant so she sat right beside us and slept all the time. It seemed like she waited to have her pups. As soon as we got to the farm in Alberta, she had them.

We were crowded and uncomfortable on the train, but somehow the young ones managed to make the whole experience seem like a wonderful adventure. We whiled away the hours playing my brother's records, exchanging jokes about the handsome cowboys riding the Alberta ranges, or just enjoying the train ride that was so exciting for many of us. But the older folks were subdued most of the way. You could see older women weeping from time to time. We tried to sleep on the hard seats with the *clickety-clack clickety-clack* of the railroad tracks. Our first sight of the majestic Rockies made us all forget for a moment why we were there.

We reached the railroad station at Calgary on the second day of our trip. A delegation from a well-known women's club met us at the station during the short stopover and demanded that we be kept on the train. The RCMP constable, who accompanied us, spoke on our behalf and after much wrangling, we were finally allowed to get off and stretch our legs. We got out to walk around a bit. It was one of those windy Alberta days, we discovered. I reached up for my fedora so I wouldn't lose it. We were told that we had another day of travel to reach Raymond and other points. We were looking forward to some hot coffee, only to be refused service in a small café.

We arrived at the Lethbridge station on a cold evening on April 14. We had to stay on board the train that night. Once again, the constable was kind enough to grant us "leave" to explore Lethbridge as long as we promised to be back at a specified hour. We were delighted to see Galt Gardens and the wide, clean streets of the city. We had heard rumours about the cold, desolate prairies with not a tree in sight and so the park was a most welcome sight for people who had just left blossoming fruit trees in B.C.

The different families were dispersed to small towns in the Lethbridge area—Coaldale, Diamond City, Picture Butte, Magrath, Raymond, Taber, Vauxhall, and others. We were met in Magrath by a group of curious farmers and their children. It seemed like they were expecting something like a circus coming to town, maybe a bunch of gypsy people with bags on their backs. But we arrived as first-class citizens. The men wore ties, sports jackets and fedoras, and the ladies were in their finery. We heard the kids say, "Look—they've got bicycles and sewing machines."

As everyone stepped off the train, the RCMP officers were directing traffic. "Your family has been assigned to the Johnson farm," the police officer instructed me. Mr. Johnson was a very nice gentleman. He took over our baggage and loaded it in his wagon and drove us out to his farm in a Model-A car. After a five-mile drive, we reached our destination that turned out to be a dirty two-room shack on top of a hill in the middle of the prairie. We were flabbergasted. It had not been cleaned out since the last tenants. It was just a shell of a one-room structure that may have been used as a bunkhouse at one time. But now it stood dilapidated and uninviting. The windowpanes were devoid of glass and there were cobwebs all over. The door was hanging on only one hinge. There was a broken-down stove, a table with three legs, two broken chairs and a couple of boxes in the corner for shelves. An old mattress, with chicken droppings on it, was propped up against one of the walls. We looked at Mr. Johnson and I said, "Sir, I am not putting my family into this hell-hole after travelling three days on a train that had better facilities. Please take us back to town. We will stay in a hotel, if there is one, till we do some renovations on this old shack."

Mr. Johnson was a fine gentleman and he understood our predicament. We piled into his little jalopy and he said that he would make room in his own home and put us up. The next day he found out that we were carpenters of a sort, so he bought some lumber and we built a lean-to on the shack, repaired all the furniture and made the place liveable. We cleaned out the old well that was stale, so he was pleased that we were capable of doing all this work.

When it came time to move in, we needed food. When we asked Mr. Johnson, he said that we could catch and harness up a team of horses from the pasture and drive the horse and wagon five miles to town. When I refused, he agreed to bring out the groceries the next day if we gave him a list. When he saw our list, he shook his head and said that we'd never make a living in the beet fields if we were going to eat like that. We told him that we ate better than that before we came there and we didn't intend to be beet workers very long.

As it turned out, we ate very poorly that spring, as we were low on cash. We thinned beets and ate a lot of the beet thinnings along with eggs, as they were only ten cents a dozen. But the price went up as soon as the storekeeper knew we were consuming them by the dozen. We sure built up the economy of that little hamlet!

In July, we experienced a terrible hailstorm on Magrath's annual day of celebration. The stadium had been full of people just a half hour before the storm struck. It took the roof off the stadium and deposited it across the street. It was only a matter of minutes, but our crop was all but destroyed. The leaves had been whipped off by the high winds. The foliage came back, but the crop was stunted. Things weren't working out very well there in Magrath, as Mr. Johnson's farm was very small and poor, so we talked about moving to a different area in southern Alberta, where we hoped that we could make a better living.

Since our earnings had been very poor that summer, the next winter I took up an opportunity to work for the Atlas Lumber Company at Rocky Mountain House. About thirty-five of us young men who had worked in the beet fields went to work in the bush and sawmill. It was very cold. Luckily, Mihoko had knitted me some leggings to take along. We had to work day and night shifts. The bunkhouses that we stayed in were built to be portable, so at night we could see the stars through the joints between the sections of the building. It was so cold that we would take our clothes for the next day, along with our jackets, and wrap them around our bodies to go to sleep. Our clothes would freeze to the walls if we weren't careful. But the food was good and we had plenty to eat. We had to work day and night until it got minus thirty degrees Fahrenheit. We worked ten hours a day. I worked in the bush felling trees until Christmas and then I got in to the sawmill where the work was more interesting.

We had to make our own fun. When a fellow had a bath at night in the washtub, some of the boys might get together and carry him outside and leave him yelling for a few seconds until he could be rescued by some of the others.

In the spring, I applied to the B.C. Security Commission and asked if our family could transfer to Taber where we could be able to make a better living. They said that they would help us monetarily if we couldn't make a living, but I told them that we didn't want to be wards of the government. Finally they said "OK," so we moved to the Jim Valgardson farm. The farmer provided us with a very big house. In the meantime, I had applied for a job at the Taber Canning Company. I got on right away in the spring, on the maintenance crew, and worked right through the pea and bean campaigns and into the early fall. When I wasn't working in the beet fields, I was working at the canning company. I worked myself up into the assistant foreman position of the warehouse.

In exchange for the lodgings on the Valgardson farm, we spent the next five years thinning, hoeing, weeding, irrigating and topping twenty-five acres of sugar beets. Thinning the beets was backbreaking work. In the spring, the beets would appear like clustered radishes. The clusters needed to be thinned out, so that only one seedling was left every one-foot apart. To achieve this, father and I went ahead and did the hoeing, while my younger sister and brother crawled behind us, to thin the plants out. The long rows seemed to go on forever.

During the growing season, only the odd weeding and irrigating was necessary. The really hard work began with the harvesting of the sugar beets. I recall standing shivering in the cold November mornings staring at the seemingly never-ending rows of full-grown sugar beets. The beet leaves by now had grown to about twelve inches or more and had a leafy appearance similar to Swiss chard. The beet portion was white, turnip-like in texture, and grew to the size of a pineapple, or even larger.

Eight rows at a time were ploughed up and loosened by a horse-drawn beet digger that pulled them up out of the ground. The beets were then pulled up by hand, four rows placed to the right and four rows to the left, leaving a clear path down the middle. A stone-board was then dragged down this opening to smooth it down. Into this area, the topped beets were thrown and kicked into line, so that a motorized pick-up implement could be used to lift up the beets and transfer them onto a passing truck. "Topping" a sugar beet was the action of hooking the beet with a C-shaped hook, which was attached to the tip of machete-like blade. Holding the beet in one hand, you hacked off the leaves. If the knife was sharp, one swift chop did the job.

Mihoko had such small and delicate hands that she couldn't grasp the sugar beet, but had to balance each one on her tiny palm. One time, she chopped off the tip of one finger. We picked up the piece of her finger and rushed her to the hospital in Taber. She had it sewn back on and today it is a little numb, but you can hardly see the scar.

I guess we were lucky that our family consisted of two adult men and my sister. Jutaro attended high school in Taber, where they had started to call him "John," and he could only help on weekends. But we heard about other families that had a lot of little kids. In the family down the road, the ten-year-old daughter was given the task of steering the three-ton beet truck. It was "governed," with the carburetor adjusted to go at a constant speed, but it was an enormous challenge for a little girl who was only able to see through the openings of the huge steering wheel. Three younger ones worked at pulling the loosened beets from the ground and shaking off any dirt, preparing them for topping. The older brothers and parents topped the beets and then tossed them into the bin of the truck.

There were all kinds of situations in the Japanese families. There were mothers who never expected to work in the soil again, old men who had looked forward to relaxing in their twilight years, young women who had had manicures and permanent waves in their hair while living back in Vancouver. They worked from dawn till dark and even by moonlight to produce a record Canadian beet crop. People had thought that girls couldn't harvest the beets. But they did. They worked alongside their family members, with the stiff southwest wind blowing stinging dust in their eyes, their fingers frozen in the cold morning frost. Then they hauled water from a hole chopped in the ice a quarter or half a mile away, and staggered back with spilling buckets, to their frame shacks with coal oil lamps, and the bare, chilly outhouse.

One of the things I learned from the whole experience was that no job was tougher than working in those sugar beet fields. We had worked in fruit and vegetables in Surrey, but nothing was like working in the sugar beets in Alberta. The pay was hardly anything. Even with all of us working for this farmer, we could barely make enough money to buy groceries. You can't call that living. It was impossible to live. All of father's savings, all the money he had saved all his life for his old age, all of it went on winter clothes and boots and things, because Alberta was so cold and we had to have warm clothing. Surrey was much warmer.

When Mihoko decided to get married and move away, John also wanted to move to Ontario and I realized that I could not make a good living on the farm with just my father and myself working. We were tired of all the hard work and looked for other ways to make a living. We didn't think about going back to the coast. In 1949 and 1950, when the restrictions were lifted, some Japanese did go back to the coast, but they were mainly fishermen. Akira and Midori decided to move back. A company that paid for their transportation sponsored him. I don't think we would have even had enough money to pay our train fare, even after all those years of working so hard.

About this time, I decided to become a carpenter. A fellow down the road, who was at logging camp with me, was a carpenter working for a contractor, so I asked him if there was a chance of getting on too. I was lucky. There was an opening so I got on as a learner, but soon I was working as a full-time carpenter. I guess my building experience from B.C. helped. I learned a lot in the couple of years that I worked for this contractor.

In the meantime, I decided to get married. I had courted a few girls around the Taber area, but there was a family down the road, the Shimazaki family, who had been part of the group of Japanese pioneers in Raymond. There was one girl in the family, Uino, whom I really liked. She had had her name changed to "Ruth" when she got baptized in the United Church in Taber. We would double date with her brother, Tosh, and my sister, Mihoko. People had shortened her name to "Mimi." We had a lot of fun going to baseball games in the area.

When we decided to get married, by Japanese custom you were supposed to have a "go-between," so we thought we'd follow the old tradition. We each asked older friends of the family to act on our behalf. Traditionally, when there were arranged marriages, the "go-betweens" would make the agreement between the parents of the bride and groom. However, in our case, it was just a formality. We asked the minister from the Raymond Buddhist Church to officiate at the Buddhist church in Dogtown. After the ceremony on a cold day in January 1947, we had a full sit-down meal of Japanese and Chinese foods. We left for a month-long honeymoon to New Westminster at the home of old family friends, the ones who had helped out my sister, Midori. When we got there, we were still under travel restriction, so we were under the care of our friends and had to report regularly to the RCMP. I helped them on their acreage and they took us around wherever we wanted to go. We had given them the truck we had on the farm when we had had to leave. It was a great holiday and we sure hated to come home again to the reality of work and cold.

We settled down to family life. We moved in with my father and brother, John, who was finishing high school. Ruth took over the cooking and cleaning, and within a year she had our first daughter. We gave her an English name for a first name and a Japanese one for her middle name: Valerie Mariko. We had another daughter and finally a son, all born in the Taber General Hospital. When our son was born, I couldn't believe that I finally had a son, so I asked the nurse if it was really a boy. She said, "Oh yes, it has a handle on it."

In 1951, restrictions were lifted that banned Japanese people from moving into Lethbridge, so we decided to move into the city. I had been working in Lethbridge with an Englishman I had met on a carpentry job. He was a very likeable person, recently over from England, and trying to get a foothold in the industry. We were both new in the city and quite compatible, so we decided that we should start a company together. There was construction work aplenty in the city. We decided to build a duplex for ourselves in our spare time. We each lived in half of the duplex with our families.

When we came out to the beet fields in Alberta, the people here were scared. They had heard about the Japanese whom they were at war with and thought that Canadian Japanese were terrible people. When they found out we were not part of the war, but were peaceful and hard working, and didn't want to cause any trouble, a lot of people changed their attitudes. There was a headline that read, "Japs Speak Slang, Know Hit Parade." Well, we had grown up in Vancouver where the slang and Glenn Miller were the same as the slang and Glenn Miller in Alberta.

We knew that we had to show that we were good people and were good citizens. We did very well. We proved that we could work hard and save our money and we were successful. No bitter feelings.

6

SANSEI

Valerie M. (Akagawa) Takahashi

I was born in Taber General Hospital, the first of six children born to my Japanese Canadian parents, who had met and married in the Taber area. We moved to Lethbridge before I started school. I remember the day that we left for Lethbridge. I witnessed a most poignant scene. I'm sure that this experience was a common one in those days, but it was so powerful for me that it will be etched in my memory forever.

I recall sitting in the back seat of my parents' newly-purchased, used 1951 Pontiac. The car was packed with the last of our luggage and was parked in front of our "beet shack," that we had called home for the past few years on a farm near Barnwell, a small village near Taber. I remember my mother and my father standing by the car, staring at our home in complete silence. As a little girl, I couldn't understand why my mother was crying as she cradled my little brother in her arms. My dad stared for a bit and then cast his eyes downward, wiping a teardrop that had emerged from the corner of his eye. They stood there for a minute or two. Finally, my dad touched my mother's shoulder. They both turned away, climbing into the car. We drove away in silence. I didn't know what was happening, except that we were moving to the big city of Lethbridge.

Over the years, I've always wondered why my parents were so upset with leaving such a hard life on the farm to live in Lethbridge, with all its wonderful opportunities. It was only years later that I came to realize what that snapshot in time really meant to me. I believe it taught me two lessons in life that are an integral part of the life of Japanese Canadians. One has to do with the past and the other has to do with the future: always be thankful and respectful of where you have come from, and always strive to better yourself through hard work.

Throughout the years, our parents have taught us many lessons. They have provided the guidance and leadership that have made the Japanese Canadians trusted and respected citizens in our community, in our province, and in our country. They made it so much easier for future generations to be successful in life. We owe them our respect, our gratitude and our very lives! However, it has taken me a long time and a lot of soul-searching to come to this point of understanding.

Several years ago, on a holiday with my own family, we visited the fishing village of Tofino, British Columbia, on the western edge of Vancouver Island. There is a sign that proclaims it the westernmost point of the Trans Canada Highway. I stood for the first time on the vast, desolate beach and looked at the huge waves breaking, one after the other on the beach. I was overcome with the realization that just one body of water, although immense, separated me from the homeland of my ancestors and my roots.

Over the years, my parents had mentioned "the coast" and a few experiences from my father and grandfather's lives there and also mentioned "the evacuation," but they did not elaborate very much, seeming to want to close the book on that chapter in their lives. Very seldom had they talked about their experiences in moving to Alberta and settling here.

I did know about my uncle having been a fisherman on the coast, with his base near Tofino, at the nearby town of Ucluelet. We had made a trip to his boat once when I was a small child, and I had had trouble walking the gangplank to get onto the boat that tossed to and fro in the water, giving me a queasy stomach. What I didn't really know was that he had been a fisherman before and after the war.

As an adult, I have read a little in history books, but it has been mostly through my own research, reading and talking to people, that I have come to an understanding of what the evacuation was all about.

On this family holiday, as we walked on the beach and collected shells, I wondered whether these same kinds of shells could also be found on the Japan side of the ocean. Then I wondered whether some of them could have come all that way to be washed ashore in Canada. Maybe like the shells, my grandparents on both sides of my family had made the journey across the water, and now as a third-generation Canadian, I still appear Japanese. The same as my parents, I was born in Canada and have been raised in a Western culture. I consider myself a full-fledged Canadian, although I often feel like I am on the edge of things. There are constant reminders that I am not and will never be, an "ordinary Canadian," whatever that might be. Ever since I was young, I have been asked questions like: "Why is your face so flat?"

It might come as a surprise to hear this, but it is only as an older adult that I have become interested in my roots in Japan. I grew up in that great "melting pot" of the 1960s in which being ethnic was not popular. There was no Alberta Heritage Day and there was little interest or appreciation for cultural differences and values. Those of Japanese descent had just barely been allowed to live within the city limits during the past decade. So looking back, I can now understand—although it was very painful at the time—to be mocked by complete strangers. One day when I was about six years old, I was walking down a Lethbridge street to go to my friend's house. I was minding my own business, when I passed by some white children who were playing on the street. They started to taunt me by calling me, "Chinky-chinky Chinaman...!" I knew they were making fun of my appearance, so my face burned with rage and humiliation, as I ran to the safe haven of home to tell my mother. She comforted me, telling me to "consider the source." I didn't quite know what she had meant at the time, except that it meant that people didn't appreciate others who looked different from them.

Up until that time, I did not realize that I looked different from anyone else. Our family spoke English, dressed in Western clothes, ate Western foods, and attended a Christian church. We lived in a duplex on the southside of Lethbridge, where few non-white immigrants lived. As I recall, there was nothing in our home to say that we were not regular Canadians. For birthday parties, my mother baked angel food cakes that had been mixed with her electric beater. The Easter Bunny visited our home and a lighted face of Santa Claus hung in our window in December. We got our first television set in 1955, on which we enjoyed watching Howdy-Doody and Maggie Muggins. The people in the other half of the duplex were from England. They were our close friends, because the father was my dad's business partner. Their teenaged daughter would babysit us and teach us songs and games. Whenever their grandma, "Nanny Best," would visit from England, she would play with me and bounce me on her ankle:

Ride a cockhorse to Banbury Cross,
To see a fine lady on a white horse;
Rings on her fingers and bells on her toes,
She will have music wherever she goes.

She called me "Lovey" and sent me taffeta hair ribbons and magazines from England once she had returned home.

What a shock then, to find that there were some people who apparently didn't like me because I had different physical features. When I was a child, I went to Sunday school at a nearby Presbyterian church where the words to a song included, *"Red and yellow, black and white, All are precious in His sight."* If those words were true, then why wouldn't people find me acceptable? It took me many years to have the courage and insight to seek answers.

I remember the first time I entered school in Lethbridge. I was awed by the hugeness of the old brick building. I vividly remember how ominous it looked after living on farms with wooden barns and old run-down shacks. The inside was just as impressive, as I stood there with my eyes glued on the shiny wooden railings and the wide winding steps that led upward toward the sky. However, the most frightening thing about the experience was the number of scary, unfriendly-looking white faces of all sizes and shapes gawking and pointing at me, as I huddled around my parents, looking for a place to hide. I guess it didn't really matter that we were dressed in our Sunday best, with our hair curled or slicked down, faces washed and shoes polished. I am sure we were a sight to behold, for I was the only Japanese student attending this school. I tried to keep to myself, but some days the name-calling got to be too much, and with a friend, who was of Chinese background and suffered similarly, we would hide under the stairs for recess break, rather than face our classmates.

I'm not sure if it was the same for Chinese people, but as Japanese people, we were trying to pretend we weren't Japanese, or that we didn't look different from anyone else. But every time we had a reminder of our differentness, we were brought back to reality. In elementary school, after the valentine card exchange each year, I would end up with a handful of the same valentines, with a picture of an Oriental girl that read, "Ah-so, will you be my valentine?" In grade six, when our class was doing a gift exchange for an old folks' home, I was chosen by the teacher from among my white classmates to give a Christmas gift to the person on the list who was named only as "Japanese." I remember having trouble buying the gift, without even knowing if it were a man or woman. I ended up buying a box of chocolates and writing on the card, "Japanese person." When I presented the gift to the elderly Japanese man, I remember him peering into my eyes in a searching way, but I was unable to understand when he talked to me. However, that searching look is one with which I am all too familiar. When I happen to meet people of Japanese origin, they often look at me in this way, trying to place my Orientalness: am I one of them, a Japanese Canadian, and have I suffered the same as them?

These incidents continued throughout my childhood and adolescence, and I even tried to deny that I was Japanese, by pretending to my friends that my second name was "Mary" and not Mariko. When I was a young adult, an elderly Englishwoman in the city of

Victoria, B.C. asked me where "my people" came from. It took me aback because this was something I had hardly ever thought about. Another time, I was in a bank in a suburb of Toronto, which happens to be the city in Canada where the largest number of people of Japanese descent live. I was asked for my passport in order to cash Canadian travellers' cheques, which normally only require a matching signature. I guess because I looked foreign, it was assumed that I was not Canadian. Ironically, I have never traveled to any country other than the United States and at the time, did not even have a passport. A hotel employee, who himself had an Asian accent, once commented that my English was very good. Even immigrants have a hard time figuring out how someone who looks like an immigrant can sound so Canadian.

I was practically a teenager before I heard the story of the evacuation. It was something that was hardly mentioned in our home and our parents didn't like to talk about it, even if they were asked directly. They would rather turn our attention to the task at hand, that of trying to fit in with the rest of the people in the community. One of the best ways to do that was through education. We were encouraged to do well in school. When we got awards or honours, however, we were then told to be humble. So, we were supposed to do our best, but not to stick out amongst others and show pride for accomplishments.

My mother loved the simple poetry of Robert Louis Stevenson and liked to present each of us with our own copy of, *A Child's Garden of Verses.*[2] It never occurred to me at that time that we were not like the fair-haired English children in the storybooks. However, you could have said we were a bilingual household, because my Japanese-speaking grandfather lived with us for thirty-five years. True to traditional Japanese culture, my grandfather lived with the family of his oldest son, my father. Although my parents spoke Japanese to my grandfather and a few older relatives and friends, they were both fully fluent in English and

---

[2] Stevenson, Robert L., *A Child's Garden of Verses* (London: George G. Harrap & Co., 1946).

there was little motivation to learn what could be called our "mother tongue."

For a few years, my younger sister and brother and I reluctantly attended "Japanese school" once a week, in the home of a tiny and serious gentleman named, Mr. Endo. (It is interesting that his son became the first Japanese Canadian teacher in the Lethbridge School District in 1951, as a "test case.") He tried to translate the words in the Japanese readers into English, but we were either puzzled or amused most of the time because of his heavy accent. It was many, many years later that we discovered that a "*pus-min*" was a "persimmon," a fruit that we had never seen in Canada anyway. We were so opposed to learning Japanese, that we agreed in our family to refer to the lessons as "J. School." The decision came about after an embarrassing incident that had occurred when some white friends were present when we had to discuss changing the time of going to our lessons. After that, we could not even bring ourselves to speak the word, "Japanese," out loud. When we told our parents that we wanted to quit, Mr.

Endo attempted to bribe us with cookies and sweets after each lesson. I am embarrassed now at my lack of respect or effort and have some regrets that I cannot understand or speak the language. I have been asked countless times whether I can speak Japanese, and when I say, "No," people usually make the comment, "That's too bad." As an older adult, I can agree with them, but as a child growing up, it was the furthest thing from my mind.

Learning another language is not just about learning new words to translate. There are some things that do not have a direct translation, because of different cultural practices. For example, the word *kyodai* in Japanese has no English equivalent (except perhaps "siblings," although most people don't use it in everyday speech) and refers to one's brothers and sisters, but it implies more than just a relationship, to include familial obligation. As an example, when we were painting our new house, my mother-in-law called all my husband's brothers and sisters to come over and help us. They came out in full force—with donuts!

I have learned more about Japanese words and customs from marrying a second-generation Japanese man, than from my own parents. His family observes more Japanese customs, since his parents came from Japan and the *Issei* community has kept many practices in a kind of time warp. Even though the Japanese in Japan change with the times, the people who have immigrated to Canada have "freeze-dried" their culture so that it stays much the same. For example, my mother-in-law still calls a woman's purse by the archaic word, *kin-chaku,* while recent visitors from Japan laughed at that usage and called it a *hando-bagu!*

Each year, at the end of the summer, my mother-in-law informs me that a particular Sunday is *Obon* ("Festival of Souls," in which the souls of ancestors are honoured and prayed for) and I make sure that I have a particularly colourful bouquet of cut flowers to place at my mother's grave. Her grave is situated in the "Japanese section" of the local cemetery and at this time of year it is a stunning sight to see the whole Japanese section ablaze with gladioli and other bright flowers. I feel a personal duty as the eldest daughter to attend to my mother's grave on a weekly basis during the spring, summer, and early fall. This makes a public statement of my love for her memory, but I also feel a strong sense of community pressure. The Japanese are known for their attention to the proper way to do things and for their respect for their elders, so an empty flower vase at my mother's grave would state to the Japanese community that I have forgotten about her and maybe never loved her, rather than that I have chosen to opt out of Japanese tradition.

Since my mother's family was Christian, we do not observe the same traditions that come from Buddhism. Buddhist tradition is based on a Chinese practice of respect for ancestors, which means attending regular services for the deceased at seven-day, hundred-day, one-year, three-year, seven-year, or longer, intervals. One summer, my mother-in-law's family gathered to observe the thirty-second anniversary of her husband's passing. Probably half the people at the service were too young (or had joined the family too late) to have ever known the man, but the *bonsan* (Buddhist teacher) tried to impress upon the family members present that we owed our present lives to this particular man, who was being remembered. To his children and grandchildren, this should have been a serious thought. In Western culture, we rarely think of the contributions of our ancestors. In fact, as a youngster growing up in white society, I had given no thought to great-grandparents who came from far-off Japan, but more often made fun of my grandfather for his eccentricities and was repelled by his religious rituals, in which we sometimes had to take part.

I remember having to bow awkwardly to the picture of our grandmother who had died even before my parents were married. Her picture was a murky, black-and-white snapshot that stood among small piles of fruit and *manju* (dessert bean and rice cakes) in the *butsudan* (ancestral altar). This shrine was kept hidden from everyday view, in my grandfather's bedroom. It was a sturdy wooden box painted shiny black, with a series of elaborate folding doors and a small, bronze bowl that sat on a brightly coloured cushion. As children, we would sometimes sneak into the room and take up the little wooden baton to make the bowl sound like a tiny gong. It was fascinating as a plaything, but held no religious meaning to us as children. Although the person honoured was my father's mother and a woman described as "wonderful," I could not understand what was so important about the woman being honoured.

As I have grown older, I have realized the importance of looking backward as well as forward. The Nikkei Cultural Society of Lethbridge and Area has recently held a *Keiro-kai* celebration for that very purpose, to honour those of eighty years of age or older, for their hard work in paving the way for future generations.

As a young child, I used to think that Buddhist services only made people sad by remembering the past. However, now I have learned as an adult, that the purpose of this practice is to remember the deceased and pray that the spirits of ancestors are at rest. In contrast,

Western culture has few formal opportunities to remember the lost loved one beyond the funeral service held immediately after the death.

I've heard that Japanese customs, beliefs and values were followed very closely on the west coast, and they helped Japanese Canadians become successful in Canada. However, after the evacuation, some Japanese Canadians have said that the dispersal across Canada has been positive, because it forced the young people to move out of ethnic ghettos. When they moved from British Columbia to other provinces, the Japanese found better opportunities, if not for themselves, then for their children. Some became teachers, nurses, lawyers, and accountants, while in British Columbia they might not have been allowed to practice these professions outside the Japanese community. In a way, through hard work and trying to fit in, they have been able to "seek their fortune" yet again.

Fitting in to the larger culture, however, has resulted in a loss of the Japanese culture for most *Sansei,* like myself. We have thoroughly adapted to the customs, values and institutions of post-war Canada. We have also intermarried with other cultural groups and scattered geographically and throughout the labour force, so much so, that we cannot be identified as a specific group. We have abandoned the language and culture of Japan, giving little everyday thought to our background or roots. However, it is this generation that has started to look back at our history and started to tell the story in public, rather than just behind closed doors. It seems that the Japanese in Canada have come to a point where we can start to hold our heads up proudly, as a people who underwent enormous emotional and physical suffering, but successfully weathered the adversity and made important contributions to Canadian society.

7

YONSEI

Mackenzie Takahashi

I was born in Lethbridge, to Japanese Canadian parents. My father is *Nisei* and my mother is *Sansei*. I have lived all my life in Lethbridge, attending public schools in the city. Yet, I cannot classify myself completely as a Canadian. Not only is my physical appearance different, but I also have many beliefs that belong to my Japanese ancestors. Even though I was born and raised in this country, many times I find myself confused about many traditions and behaviours. I find that I have to try to change my behaviours and my way of thinking in order to survive.

I didn't think much about analyzing my heritage until my English teacher in grade twelve practically insisted that for a novel study, I should read *Obasan*, by Joy Kogawa, although it wasn't my first choice. I had started reading *Wuthering Heights*, but I found it really boring, so I asked if I could have my second choice, *Catcher in the Rye*. He said I had to read *Obasan*, even though he didn't insist that anyone else in the class had to read a certain book. I'm pretty sure it was because I was Japanese. My white friend asked for *Catcher in the Rye* as a second choice and she got it, and he still had a copy left to give me, but he wouldn't give it to me.

So, I wasn't very enthusiastic from the start, but it took me many weeks to read the novel and it disturbed me so much that I couldn't bring myself to even finish reading it. The topic of the Japanese Canadian internment was really hard for me to deal with. If you looked at me, you would see a Japanese person, but sometimes I forget how others see me. When I look in the mirror each morning, it is not a Japanese girl I see, but rather I see an ordinary person. As I read the book, it was a constant reminder to me of how different I was from a regular white Canadian. What had happened in the past to my ancestors had happened *because* they were different, at least in outward appearance.

In *Obasan*, the main character, Naomi, reads the journal that her Aunt Emily kept at the time of the evacuation of the Japanese Canadians during the Second World War. The novel gives an intense inside look at the pain and confusion that the Japanese Canadians felt during the time of the evacuation. Those feelings were passed on to me as I read this book. Because I shared the same ancestry, I could not be just a casual reader. But years after the evacuation, I too have felt the harsh whip of racism. I ended up writing an essay that I called, "Longing to belong."

I am a third-/fourth-generation Japanese Canadian. When I am driving in my car, walking in the mall, or working in class, I do not think of myself as different in any way. I still do not see myself as any different from the girl next to me, the same way that Naomi felt as a child. Naomi, as I do now, did not feel as though she was different until it was pointed out to her. I think many children of visible minorities feel the same feelings as Naomi. Joy Kogawa felt like an outcast when her classmates pointed out that she was different. In a poem she wrote:

> *Then the war was over but Lorraine*
> *And her friends spat on us anyway*
> *And I prayed to the God who loves*
> *All children in his sight*
> *That I might be white.*

I, too, have often wished that I looked like everyone else. I wish I could blend in, when in a group. Instead, my black hair stands out in a sea of blonde hair.

I got some blue-coloured contact lenses and at first, it was a novelty, until people would point out how I could not possibly actually have blue eyes. According to the laws of genetics, it is true that it is not possible, unless one of my parents had blue eyes—and we all know that all Japanese have black hair and brown eyes. I don't think people are saying these things to make me feel bad or like an outsider. Yet, it is just another notice handed to me that I am not like them.

I often hear the question, "So, are you Japanese or Chinese?" and I think to myself, "Is it that important that they know what cultural background I am from?" The other question that is asked of me, and is also asked of Naomi in *Obasan*, "How long have you been in this country?" How often do people ask a white person with no accent how long they have lived in the country? I doubt that it would happen very often. I go to a mainline Christian church. A girl at a youth event at my church once asked if I only found Oriental guys attractive. The question was a shock to me. I had never been asked that and I had never even thought of it. I do not look at people by what race they are, but rather by the person's personality. I am not one to discriminate, because I know what it is like to be the victim.

When I was in elementary school, there was a boy who would call me "*sushi*" or "raw fish" every day at recess. The name-calling did not really bother me, but I tried to explain to him that he was calling me two separate things. I tried to teach him about Japanese food. I decided that if he was going to make fun of me, he should at least have his facts straight. My lesson never seemed to help, because he would argue with me about what *sushi* really was. After eating it for a good portion of my life, I thought that maybe the boy would believe me! When that tactic failed, I would tell him that he was a "bigot." The grade four boy had no clue what it meant and therefore was stumped. My mother actually had given me the advice. She told me that he would not know what the word meant and would have to ask his mom what it meant. His mother would ask him why, and he would have to tell her that it was because a girl at school was calling him that. Once I started calling him a bigot, he would ask me what it meant and every time I would tell him to ask his mom. I am not sure if he ever did tell his mom, or if he just gave up teasing me for another reason.

That was an example of an easier time when I was faced with an ignorant mind. There have been plenty of other times when I have had to be strong when I faced others who were not open-minded. When I was five years old, I was at my uncle's Christian church in Coaldale where a Chinese boy about my age began to call me names: "fat, little, Chinese boy." Of course, this did not make any sense to me, since I was not fat, Chinese, or a boy, but it still hurt. Now, when I think about it, he must have been saying to me what he had probably heard so many times said to him. He was projecting his anger onto me from all the times that he was ridiculed with those exact words.

Another time I faced prejudice was in junior high school, when a boy would tease me and call me a "*sumo* wrestler." It made me angry and it hurt me. After all, he was calling me a gigantic man who has a funny haircut! He was not only poking fun at my weight, but also at my heritage. Personally, I would prefer to watch a *sumo* wrestling match than a World Wrestling Federation wrestling match. *Sumo* wrestlers begin by doing a ceremony that is quite spiritual, rather than threatening and yelling at each other before they start to act out a fight scene that is scripted and has been practiced all week.

Prejudice continues into adulthood and pops up in the most unlikely places. Once, as an eighteen-year-old, I went down to the police station in Lethbridge to report my passport being lost. My mother and I, both speaking in perfect English, let the young officer know our reason for being there. To our surprise, he asked if we could write in English to fill out the form. I guess what he heard with his own ears did not fit with what he saw before his eyes.

I feel like I handled those and other situations quite well, simply because I either did not care or would not give bullies the satisfaction of knowing that they had hurt me. I do not know if I would have been able to survive the evacuation though. I still do not understand how the white people, and all the other people in Canada, could not see that what they were doing was wrong. Even after the war, in March 1948, the House of Commons voted that anyone of Japanese origin was not allowed to live on the coast of British Columbia or enter the province for another year, without a permit from the RCMP. Many people did not see Japanese Canadians as Canadian citizens, because physically they looked different from white Canadians. Canada did not round up all the German Canadians and herd them into barns. Why were they not treated as Japanese Canadians were? Didn't they come from another country that Canada was at war with? Or, were they not seen as a threat, since their skin and hair colour were the same as their British neighbours? Were the Japanese any different from the Germans as potential threats, besides their appearance?

In British Columbia, before WW II, Asians were often seen as a lower class than whites and therefore some of the ignorant believed that the Japanese were being treated as they deserved. The Japanese were seen as being inferior and so must be paid less for their work. But the Japanese did not complain about the lower wages. Rather, they were superior workers, compared to those around them, working harder and having a higher productivity. In Japanese culture, Japanese are taught not to complain, but rather to sacrifice for the good of the whole group. Also, they are not supposed to burden others with their own problems. I sometimes hesitate to ask for help, even in class. I do not want to bother the teacher or classmate for them to help me, or answer a question. When the *Obasan* character, Naomi, is on a train, she hears of a young woman, Kuniko-san, who had just given birth to a premature baby. "She has nothing...not even diapers."[3] Yet, Kuniko-san does not complain or beg others for anything. It is not honourable to beg from others. Honour is very important in the Japanese culture. It does not just apply to the individual person, but to the whole family.

Honour is still a strong component in the Japanese Canadian culture today. I worry about bringing any dishonour to my family by getting a bad mark or simply failing a task. I feel as though I bring shame to my family when I do not win, or I am not living up to others' expectations. I am confused by the concept of honour, yet it is ingrained in my behaviour and thoughts. Still, I am the most liberal in my family. I

---

[3] Joy Kogawa, *Obasan* (Markham, ON: Penguin Books, 1981) 113.

live "on the edge" by being part of the teenage norm and having a messy room, something that is not really acceptable in our household. However, when preparing for company coming to the house, my room must be cleaned. We must present a "proper" house. I sometimes don't understand why it is so important to have the house so clean. After all, it is mostly just my relatives coming over. Do they really judge us by whether there is dust on the furniture, or how neatly our clothes are put away? I hope that is not so.

I feel like I am torn between two cultures. I do not fit the mould of either the Japanese or the Canadians. As a person of Japanese descent, the way I act and think goes against many beliefs of my traditional culture. First, I am not very honourable. I do have some sense of honour, yet it is nothing compared to my brother's. He brings glory to the family name and lives up to the success that my father, mother, sister and numerous aunts and uncles have had, through various kinds of achievements. Yet, I fall short of that glory. Not only do

I not bring very much honour to my family, as they would wish, but I also do not behave very Japanese-like. In spite of myself, I have many Japanese behavioural traits, although they are probably not as strong as with other generations of Japanese Canadians. I have been well-disciplined and have learned what is right and wrong. I am quite obedient with authority figures such as teachers, because I am respectful, and slightly fearful, of those in power. I have learned to have gratitude for what I have and for whatever I receive. I cannot recall a time that I have not said "thank you" to a person who gave me a compliment, did me a favour, served me at a restaurant or store, or even made a simple gesture, such as opening a door for me or handing me an object. Surely these simple courtesies lend me an air of being respectful to all, bringing "honour" to my family and heritage, on a daily basis.

I recently read a list of the typical cultural traits of a Japanese person: fear of power, insecurity, obedience, cliquishness, and inability to make forceful, independent decisions. What stuck out was "insecurity." It is true that all teenagers have some insecurity about themselves and especially with girls, it is their appearance. I have the same insecurities as any teenager but more so, because I do not fit in and also because I was taught never to brag. I learned to try to curb my self-confidence. Whenever I win or accomplish something, I feel distress when I even want to express my joy. I feel as though I am bragging, something a Japanese person should never do.

It is not only that I am different in appearance from the girl next to me. I believe that I am still not seen as a Canadian. Yet, on speaking with a Japanese exchange student, he would not consider me Japanese either. I asked, "If I am not Japanese, then what am I?" He told me I was Japanese Canadian. It is a category all on its own, yet it is not a category at all to me. When I went to Japan for a school trip with a group of high school students from Lethbridge, I felt stuck between two worlds. My classmates saw me as Japanese and assumed I knew everything about Japan, yet to our

Japanese counterparts, I was a Canadian. Although many other kids surrounded me, I still felt very isolated.

My parents try to help with my struggle by saying I am in the same group as them as Japanese Canadians. Yet, my father was brought up strictly Japanese, whereas my mother was brought up with a mother who had more white influences, but a father who was quite set in his Japanese roots. You would expect that I would be more Japanese in many ways, since my mom had both Japanese and Canadian influences growing up and my father was strictly Japanese in his values and behaviours. But living in Canadian society does have a strong effect on me. I have learned how to survive in this world. I have realized that I can no longer be the passive character that is characteristic of being Japanese.

For example, in the grocery store, my mother has trouble trying to walk past people who are blocking the aisle. She would prefer to wait until people choose to move on their own, rather than sneaking past or asking to be able to step by. I, on the other hand, take a bolder tactic and squeeze past. My approach is a combination of both Japanese and Canadian. Some Canadians would walk in-between others while I simply go behind them and say "excuse me" as I walk past. I have learned to be more aggressive because if I did not, I would miss out on many opportunities. When I was in kindergarten, I would not complain about not getting served something first. The rowdy kids would receive everything first and I was always purposely waited on last. I never understood why I was practically being punished for behaving and being patient, although I was told that I was left to the end because I was patient, and thanks for being such a good girl.

Also, I have trouble saying "no" to people. I was taken advantage of many times because kids soon learned that they could get something for nothing when asking me for things. I gave away many portions of my snacks at recess time in elementary school. I thought it was rude to say "no." In junior high, it was less a case of people asking for a candy or a potato chip, but instead, they asked for gum or money. In high school, I find friends and acquaintances asking me to "lend" them a dollar. I have handed out many loonies and only a handful has ever been returned to me. Now I have learned to say "no." I lend a dollar to a friend only if I know I will get paid back. If I did not, I probably would not have any money for myself. I feel greedy thinking of myself first, but I have learned that in Canadian society, if I do not, no one else will.

I have many questions about my own identity and I have recently learned, from talking with my mother, that my one grandfather owned a strawberry farm in Surrey that would have been worth millions of dollars today. The family had to leave their successful farm and was never given any money for their crops, their land, or their animals. Then they had to come to southern Alberta and work as labourers on the sugar beet farms. No one in the family talks about this very much, but it makes me angry to think about it. I feel really strange. I feel like part of the group of people that suffered and part of the group that made them suffer. I do not understand how I can be of two cultures yet never truly feeling as though I belong to either.

Feeling like such an outsider, I have tried to explore the Japanese culture a little. Recently, I had the opportunity to attend a conference in Ontario, sponsored by the National Association of Japanese Canadians, for youth leaders of the future. While there, I was able to meet many other young people of Japanese origin and mixed blood. One of our speakers was from Lethbridge, a man I had never met before. He was half Japanese and talked about what it's like to be part of two cultures, but in a different way from my experience. I talked to him a bit after the session and found out that he had been a friend of my father's in high school in Lethbridge. I found out that there are many variations to being Japanese Canadian and each one of us has a story to tell.

I also took *karate* lessons when I was young. I was surprised to see so many white kids there and even one of our black-belt teachers was a tall, six-foot white guy who surprisingly had a Japanese accent. I learned a lot about Japanese culture from *karate* lessons because our *sensei,* or teacher, was from Japan, and he would give us lectures about respecting our parents and teachers, and never starting fights. He said we should only use *karate* as a defense, but the best defense against attack is to run. It seems like it's in our culture to try to do everything possible not to fight.

8

HAPA

Robert Toyama

I was born in 1947 in the old Galt Hospital in Lethbridge that is now the Sir Alexander Galt Museum. My great-grandfather was a farmer who came from Okinawa in 1908 to work for the Canadian Pacific Railway and later in the No. 6 coal mine in Coalhurst and Hardieville. He wanted to make enough money to buy more land in Okinawa to retire in comfort. Unlike most of the Japanese immigrants who shared this dream, he actually succeeded in meeting this goal.

My grandfather was also an *Issei*. He was already married in Japan, but came to Canada in 1917, leaving his wife and infant son to come over three years later. She was twenty-two years old, with a three-year-old son, when they arrived in Alberta after a long, hard journey from Okinawa. She had had to stay in Yokohama for a few months, waiting for a passport, before the trip to Victoria. When she finally landed in Victoria, she had to wait several days for the arrival of her husband because of a bad snowstorm. Fortunately, she was able to stay with family friends in Victoria. Then after a long, tedious train ride to Alberta, she arrived in Hardieville. It was a thriving village of over one thousand people in the 1920s and 30s, where one of the bigger mines in southern Alberta was located. Almost all of the Japanese in southern Alberta were employed in that coal mine. Most of them dreamed that they would become rich and return to Japan, but in reality, the majority worked hard in the mines and farms, but never did return to Japan to live there again.

Working in the coal mines was dangerous and often not a steady enough source of employment, so after a few years, the Toyama family decided to take up farming. After renting land for several years, they were able to buy a quarter-section of land about six miles from Lethbridge, in Sunnyside. There were thirteen children in the family, so there were lots of farm hands. But the work of the women in the family was hard because of the innumerable tasks that they had to undertake. With all those children, the first eight were boys and so when the first girl came along, grandma was very pleased that she might have some help with the household chores. They mostly raised vegetables and grain, but also had some horses, pigs, and occasionally a cow. Nobody wanted to milk the cow, which resulted in more than a few squabbles.

My father was a *Nisei,* born in Canada. He attended school at Hardieville, then Lethbridge Collegiate Institute for high school, and Garbutts Business College in Lethbridge. He worked on the family farm until he volunteered for the Canadian Army. He was the adventurous one in the family, and so in 1939, he and a friend hopped the freight train and went to Calgary to join the Royal Canadian Air Force.

They hoped to become "gunners," but failed because of their eyesight. The following year at twenty years old, he joined the army and took his basic training at Petawawa, ON. He was a member of the Royal Canadian Ordnance Corps and was sent to Camp Borden, in Sussex, England in 1941, where he used his typing and office skills as a records clerk. He was still overseas in Britain when the war in the Pacific broke out. It was ironic that both he and his older brother were already part of the Canadian army before the Canadian government disallowed Japanese Canadians in the army. His brother had been born in Japan, but had been conscripted into the Canadian Army and my father had enlisted before Pearl Harbor.

It is an interesting story as to how my parents met and it makes you want to believe in fate. The people who lived across the road from our farm in Alberta asked my dad to visit their relatives in Aberdeen, Scotland, if he got a chance during the war. He did make the visit and on his way back to Camp Borden, he spent a few days in Edinburgh where he met a friend of my mother's at a Servicemen's Canteen. Since the friend had to work, she asked my mother to act as a tour guide for my dad and that is how they met. My father would never have been in Edinburgh except for the war and my mother would never have been in Edinburgh, except for the bombing in London that resulted in her being transferred back to her hometown.

Both families were opposed to the marriage. The Japanese Canadian side thought that my mother really didn't know what she was getting into, not only marrying into a Canadian family, but a large Japanese family. My father was the first of many in his family to marry a non-Japanese, but my father was the first and I'm told that I am the oldest person who is half-Japanese living in the Lethbridge area. My mother's family thought it was the end of the world for her, not only to go halfway across the world, but also to marry one of "the enemy." I heard that my grandmother was devastated. She cried and cried, and even talked about killing herself.

After my parents were married, my mother transferred back to London where she worked for a customs and excise firm as a filing clerk. She lived with her parents in Essex and commuted to London to work and to see my father whenever possible. Those were very scary times. They had many near misses from the German Luftwaffe bombs nearby and many homes were damaged. But despite the heavy bombing, people tried to keep up with their ordinary lives, taking the attitude that if they were meant to get hit, they would be, whether out on the streets or cowering in fear at home.

After the war, my father arrived back in Alberta in late 1945 and bought a farm across the road from the family farm, using his Veteran's Grant. My mother came to Canada several months later on the *HMS Aquitania*. The ship was full of war brides, with massive seasickness from a rough five-day voyage. They were also worried about stray mines that might still be floating in the ocean or even the possibility of hitting icebergs. Some of the women were having second thoughts about going to Canada. It was one thing to fall in love with a handsome young soldier in uniform on one side of the ocean, but much less romantic to arrive in a small, backwater town "in the middle of nowhere," after having lived in big cities all your life.

I was the older of two children. My sister and I thought of ourselves as Japanese and were always accepted by the Japanese community. But we knew we were different. For one thing, we couldn't speak any Japanese, since no Japanese was spoken in the home because my mother couldn't understand. That was probably the biggest difference. We only lived half a mile away from my grandparents and I spent a lot of time there. The Japanese language was around all the time, but I understood very few words, except for words about food and my grandmother shaking her finger and saying, "*Abu-nai-yo!*" which meant, "Be careful!" as I was busy doing what little boys do.

My mother contracted polio when I was very young and she was incapacitated for about a year. My dad did whatever he had to do to keep the household running, like washing diapers and cooking meals, while she was convalescing at home. But when other Japanese people visited, he wouldn't do those things, because it's not the Japanese way for men to do women's household chores. But I don't recall there being any tension in the home. They would have ordinary arguments like any married couple, but I don't remember any conflict about cultural beliefs.

My mother did receive backlash from time to time because she was married to a Japanese guy. I remember her telling me about one time that there was this travelling saleswoman who came in the house and started giving her sales talk, showing her products, and then when she started taking the order, she wrote down our family name. Then she stopped and said, "Is this a Japanese house?" When my mother said, "Yes," she packed up her samples and walked out of the house and never came back. My mother had a lot of experiences where she would get a "double-take" when people would first meet her. From her name, they would be expecting a Japanese woman and would be surprised or confused by her Scottish face. One time in elementary school, my mother came to my class and I said to a friend, "That's my mom." He started arguing with me that it couldn't be my mother, as if I didn't even know my own mother. But that's what kids were like. Those were the days of "Father Knows Best" on television, and I guess they just couldn't feature an inter-racial marriage.

When I was younger, people were always asking me what I was, but now that I'm older, I don't view it as any of their business. In the summertime, when I was a kid, I would go into town for swimming lessons and would get really tanned. Kids would think I was Native, and they'd call me an Indian. I would proudly say, "I'm not Indian, I'm Japanese." I was also called "Jap," just like any other Japanese kid. There never was a problem with any other kids' families that I knew of, although my sister did have one bad experience. When she was a teenager, she hung around in a group of four friends. Two of them were Japanese, including my sister. One time they went to somebody's house and the parents didn't want to let them in because of the Japanese girls.

My sister could hear the mother yelling through the window. But I never had any problems dating white girls and my sister and I both married white partners. We never had any pressure to go one way or the other, by either my mom or dad.

On the farm, I played with all white kids and didn't have any trouble fitting in. I moved into Lethbridge around the age of seventeen. I had been going to high school in town for a while before I moved and I started hanging around with a lot of Japanese guys. The group wasn't exclusively Japanese. There were a lot of white guys with us too and we all got into trouble together. I guess I was a lot taller than most of them, even the white guys. I found out later that it is called "hybrid vigour." I didn't think about it at the time, but the Japanese kids were five-foot two and three and there I was, "knocking on six foot." I must have stuck out, but they never made me feel different. I never sensed anything of that sort.

Food is about the only thing that our family maintains for Japanese traditions. We had Japanese food and then we had Scottish *finnan haddie*. It was just kind of a strange diet. My mother had to learn to eat with chopsticks adeptly, otherwise she'd have starved. She learned how to cook Japanese food. She was very, very resilient. She was scared, I suppose, but she stuck it out. She loved my dad. My grandparents got used to it all and eventually, my Scottish grandparents even came to live with us on the farm. When my mother got polio, it didn't work out, so they went to live with another daughter in Ottawa. I think they got to kind of like dad after a while. He was quite outgoing. Eventually, our family decided to sell the farm and open a dry goods store. My dad knew a lot about kids. He had a special place in the back of the store for my friends and me to hang out after school, while I was supposed to be working in the store.

For religion, my father was Christian, but our family was pretty well split half and half, Christian and Buddhist. My father was associated with the First United Church in Lethbridge, probably because of the history of the United Church being the only mainstream

Christian church that took a public stand against the relocation. We weren't a very religious family. I don't feel uncomfortable in either Christian or Buddhist services. I went to those six-hour Buddhist funerals when I was a kid. It seems to alternate, with one member of the family getting married in one church and then the next one getting buried in the other, so I just "go with the flow." As time goes on, I don't feel like I'm leaning one way or the other and feel totally comfortable in each one.

In some ways I feel like I've got the best of both worlds. I have a lot of Japanese qualities, but I feel it's tempered. I'm an over-achiever, but I don't take it to such an extreme length like so many Japanese people do with their kids. Dad was very much like that. If I got eighty percent in school, I "got heck" for not getting ninety, and if I got ninety, I got heck for not getting one hundred percent. Nothing was ever good enough and I think that affected me. But I think a lot of Japanese fathers are like that. That is, you strive for excellence all the time. I don't think my parents ever had a difference of opinion over it. I think I would have remembered if they had had arguments that were of a deep nature like that. It would have stuck out as being different from the daily rhythm of living.

My parents were one of the first inter-racial marriages in southern Alberta, but when I was a kid I never realized it. I found this out when I was in my twenties. It was never thrown up at me or mentioned to me. My parents must have got looks or stares, but I don't recall. The Japanese people were very accepting and there were never any comments made, although there may have been an undercurrent somewhere, because being transplanted people, the Japanese tended to talk about people in their little community. As the years went by, the Japanese people just came to accept inter-racial marriages and I guess it was even part of their culture, to try to fit in with the dominant group.

I know people my age who had trouble, though. One of my Japanese friends was in love with a white girl and they went together for a few years, but her parents wouldn't let them get married. The couple decided that they had no choice but to split up and they each married someone else, but after a few years it didn't work out for either of them and they each got divorced and finally married each other after all. By that time, I guess there was more acceptance by her parents, when they could see that she was never happy in her first marriage.

Our family was a little different from most of the other Japanese people in southern Alberta to start with, because we were Okinawan and also we were already here in Canada. We didn't get relocated. Our diet, being Okinawan, is actually different from that of the mainstream Japanese, like having pigs' feet soup with *kombu* (seaweed). Most Japanese people don't use much pork in their diet and they would say, "What's that?" Our experience was unique, although we got tied into the whole Japanese Canadian discrimination experience. When my dad came back from the war, he had to report to the Chief of Police in Lethbridge as an enemy alien. We weren't allowed to vote or open a business. We had these rights before, but they were taken away because of the evacuation. My dad didn't seem bitter or angry. I think there was acceptance of the relocated people by the pioneers, although the Okinawans had their own little enclave.

Okinawans were always outsiders, even in Japan. I guess it was something like people from Newfoundland here. That's why they emigrated, because they weren't actually accepted in Japan. They were looked down upon by the rest of the mainland Japanese, mainly because of their reputation as owners of piggeries. It was an occupation that was despised, like butchers, tanners, and shoemakers of the old days. They were looking for a brighter future and that's why they came here. But then when all of this happened, we never felt any bad feelings for the mainland Japanese.

The Okinawan group was mostly based around a baseball team called the Coaldale Cubs. There were mostly Okinawan guys on the team and then they sort of built a little club, and had parties and picnics, and all that sort of thing. It wasn't an exclusionary thing. It was already going when the relocation happened and there was no reason to disband it. I get the sense that there was a huge amount of sympathy for the people who were relocated. We were "all in the same boat" in regard to losing our human rights.

I don't think about being Japanese on a day-to-day basis, but I do find myself being very impatient with racist attitudes. I'm sometimes overly vocal about it if I hear racist comments, not just against the Japanese, but also against anybody. People say ignorant things from time to time, and in my work in various managerial positions, I've had to tell people not to do that. I've never had to take a formal stance against racism, but I would have no hesitation to do so.

I think the important thing that's come out of this is that I'm very intolerant towards intolerance. I've never really wished that my life could have been different. I've looked at what the Japanese went through. They had so many disadvantages and things to overcome, and look what they did with themselves. They have become successful in all different kinds of areas. I'm really proud of my Japanese heritage and the struggles that we, as a people, have overcome. It might be because I was a pioneer, but I've never felt a sense of shame about being Japanese. But it has affected our whole family politically. None of our family would ever vote Liberal because of Louis St. Laurent's role in the evacuation. That's one thing that's carried over, one bit of resentment. Japanese are accepting people, but there had to have been some hard feelings somewhere.

I know that when my dad was overseas, my grandfather built up a very successful vegetable farm and he wanted to start up a vegetable market in Lethbridge. My grandfather was just an Okinawan peasant, but he was a really smart man. He was a street-smart kind of guy. But he wasn't allowed to follow his dream, because Japanese weren't allowed to open up businesses in the City of Lethbridge. So that's got to have affected my dad, that they wouldn't let his father open a business. Then on top of that, to have to go and report to the police after you served six years in the army for your country. It must have been painful, but Japanese men don't talk very much and I never talked to him about it. He died when I was quite young and I was too busy living my own life at the time. If he were alive today, we would have been able to talk about things like that.

9

NEW IMMIGRANT

Matasuke Kuno

I was born on a farm near a small village in southern Okinawa. My parents had seven children, four boys and three girls. I was the second youngest, the third son. I had been helping my father and mother on the farm since I was five or six years old. They grew sugar cane and sweet potatoes, but mostly sugar cane. The farm work became my job too. When I finished school every day, I had to come home right away. I had a snack and changed clothes and then had to go out to the field right away. Of course the weekend was no different and we worked long hours in the fields on Saturdays and Sundays. But I didn't mind too much, because everybody in the village and in the family worked the same way.

I used to look at my father's back. He couldn't stand up straight from bending over all the time. My parents never had time to take the kids to soccer or baseball, or camping, or holidays. What we did was just work. I respected my father so much because he didn't have too much, but he didn't ask anything for himself or his wife. They just concentrated on raising kids and giving them some education. When I was in grade seven, I said to my father, "Father, I'm going to be a farmer when I grow up and I'm going to help you. I'm going to give you a hand and we're going to have a good farm." So when I went to high school, I chose an agriculture high school, to learn to be a better farmer. Then just before I finished grade eleven, I learned about one of those programs where a person could work in Canada for two years to learn about farming. There used to be a program for the Southern Alberta Japanese

Potato Farmers' Association, an agreement between the Canadian and the Japanese governments. They sponsored young Japanese people to come to Canada and learn about farming for a couple of years.

My parents didn't want me to go to Canada, so far away. They figured immigration meant that it's just like many from Okinawa who went to South America and those people wouldn't be coming home for many, many years because it's so far away. So they thought Canada was the same way and they didn't want me to go. But at the same time, they didn't want to prevent me from taking the opportunity. They wanted to give me a chance to be able to open up my own eyes. I told them, "This program says after two years you can come back, or you can do anything."

The program was a good experience for me, when I look back now. I learned a lot about farming by working very hard as a farm labour in Canada. Without that kind of hardship, I could not make a good life in Canada. The program started in 1969, and I think, went until 1977 or 1978. Altogether around three hundred eighty people came. I came in the third group in 1971 and we had fifty-three or fifty-five people from Hokkaido and other parts of northern Japan, as well as other prefectures and islands of Japan. About half the people went back to Japan and about half stayed here after their program was over.

I came to Canada at the end of March and went to a farm near Picture Butte on April 1st. There was already one person from Okinawa on the farm, who came to Canada on the same program. He came in 1970. We talked about how we were going to work hard for our farm owner and make his farm much bigger, from five hundred acres to one thousand acres, because he was a Japanese person and we wanted him to be successful. But it was very hard work. I tried so hard, but I got homesick and I started to count the days, "Only six hundred more days and then I can go home." One day I saw the ducks flying up in the sky. I wished I could fly away too, back to Japan.

The farmer I worked for came from Japan to southern Alberta when he was very young. Some other people worked for evacuees. They would tell us, "You guys never had hardship like we had. This is nothing compared to what we had." They would tell us stories about what happened thirty or fifty years ago with the evacuation and coming to Alberta to work on the sugar beets. It was very hard work and not much money.

We had to pay to stay on the farm. I had to pay for airfare to come here in the first place. Back then in 1971, I made one hundred and eighty-five dollars a month on the farm. They took taxes off and then we had to pay for food. We had to cook for ourselves. We lived in a small house on the farm, not with the owner. But I knew some workers who lived in the farmhouse on the other farms. Ours wasn't a very nice house. It was just for seasonal workers. Every morning when I got up, I had to take the bed sheet and shake it outside because there were mouse droppings everywhere. But that's OK. You can't help that. It's like that on any farm. But in the wintertime, it was so cold. We had no bathroom inside. I had to go outside, just a small outhouse, no heat or anything. I got to have a shower only once a week, even in the summertime. It was especially bad at harvest time. At harvest time, we started work around seven or seven-thirty in the morning and we worked till the next morning, till two or three o'clock. Working in Japan was nothing like here. Of course, we worked very late, but we never worked seven o'clock until two or three the next morning. When I was finished each day, I was covered with dirt, but I was so tired that all I did was wash my face and just lie down. We worked seven days a week, and by the end of the week, you should have seen my sheets—you could see the shape of my body where I laid down.

I left the farm just before two years was over. I found out there were courses at the Lethbridge Community College, in English as a Second Language. I wasn't planning to stay in this country beyond two years, but I had to stay because I didn't have any money to go home. I was going to see the country and learn agriculture here and then I was going to go back and work with my father. That was my goal. So after about two years, I had no money so I said, "I have to go to town. I have to make money to pay for my airfare." Then I said, "To go to town and make a living, I have to learn English." After being in Canada for almost two years, I still couldn't speak any English because all we did was talk Japanese on the farm. The ESL course started from the beginning of the year, so I left the farm at the end of December.

But I had a good time on the farm. I enjoyed farming, especially around harvest time, when I saw nice potatoes coming up from the ground. It made me feel so good about it. The farmer's wife was very kind. She came here from Japan when she was an adult, but the farmer grew up here in Canada. His wife would try to make us feel more at home. Sometimes she would cook something nice for us. Many times I said, "I'm going to try harder because of her."

Another reason why I moved to Lethbridge was because of the Lethbridge Okinawan Cultural Society. There were six people who came from Okinawa two years before me. They came to pick us up and took us to Lethbridge to a welcome supper that the society had for us. They just opened their arms to me and to those people who came, only because we came here from Okinawa. We weren't related to anybody. They didn't know us yet, but they welcomed us just because we came from Okinawa. So that's one big thing why I moved to Lethbridge. All those Okinawan people said, "Come for breakfast, come for lunch. If you need anything, please come and ask us anything." So it was just like my father and my grandparents. It was very nice. I came here and I stayed with some of us from Okinawa. We rented one big house and we just stayed there, sometimes six, and sometimes ten, people in one house. I went to college for two months and then my money ran out. I didn't know how to apply for student loans or grants.

I decided to go to work in the Crowsnest Pass for CP Rail, as a section man. I stayed there four months until a big accident happened. My cousin was coming to pick us up and got in a car accident. It bothered me so much that I didn't want to stay there anymore. He was not actually my cousin. I had an auntie living in

Winnipeg, my father's sister. Her husband's sister's family was related to people in the Crowsnest Pass. So I started calling them "uncle, auntie and cousins," even though they weren't really my close relatives. Uncle was working at CP Rail and that's why I got the job. After that I came to Lethbridge and I worked for a very short time building trailers. Then I started working at a meat plant. That was the only place I could work, because I couldn't speak English. Many Japanese people were working there at that time. I learned to cut meat. It was so boring, all day every day the same thing. But I couldn't believe how much money I made for just eight hours of work. Every month I was able to send fifty dollars to my parents in Japan. That was a lot of money at that time. They were very happy and appreciated it very much.

When Japanese people first came to this country, they had to work for very low wages. They didn't get the same pay as other Canadian people. But they worked hard and didn't complain, so now Canadian people respect them. By the time I came to Lethbridge, I could make the same wages as any other Canadian. I was talking to an RCMP officer one day and he said he's never seen any crime with Japanese Canadians. In my heart I say "thank you" to all those people who worked so hard in Canada a long time ago. They made it so much easier for all of us. Even now, I go to funerals of older Japanese people to thank them and to show appreciation for their hard work in gaining respect from Canadians. We shouldn't forget this.

When I moved to Lethbridge, I could feel people here looking at my friends and me a little differently. Of course, it was our fault too, because when we got together to go out to eat or drink, we spoke Japanese all the time and were so loud. We were ten Japanese boys and only young kids, not afraid of anything. When we went anywhere, we acted like the room belonged to us, making a lot of noise. There were many times when I thought we would get into a fight. One guy in our group had learned *karate* in Japan and was teaching *karate* already when he moved to Lethbridge. He said to us, "If I start punching somebody, I know how hard I can punch and I know how hard I can kick. I can hurt them. But if I hurt someone, what are people going to think? I'm sure Canadian people would never just say that I did it. They are going to say Japanese people did it. For myself, I can't do that. I can't put all Japanese people down because of me. I can't use my fists."

One time, we went for a drink and went to a restaurant for supper and were talking Japanese. We were twenty-one or twenty-two years old. Two Canadian girls came in and sat down not far away. Then two boys came in after and sat down near them. We saw that those boys kept looking at the girls and wanted to get their attention. So they started talking. We couldn't understand what they were saying, but they kept looking at the girls and one guy said, "*Bonzai.*"

Then one of us said, "They're picking on us. They're making fun of us."

Then the Canadian boys said, "*Kamikaze.*"

The girls didn't want to see them. They didn't want to see us either. They knew what was going to happen.

One of my friends said, "That's it." He stood up.

But our friend who knew *karate* said, "Sit down, don't go," and grabbed him and made him sit down. He said, "Listen, I'll talk to them." He went over and said, "I know you guys were just joking, but do you know me? I don't know you. A joke means we know each other and we can joke around with each other. But you don't know us and we don't know you. That's not joking anymore. Would you do me favour? Say sorry to my friends and then we don't have to do anything." So they just said sorry and took off.

Many times the same thing happened to me. When I was working at the meat plant, this guy came and started punching me on the arm. I said, "Yes?"

He said, "I want to fight today. I want to beat up somebody. Let's go outside."

I said, "I don't want to fight. If I did something wrong, I'm sorry, but I don't want to fight."

"Come on, let's go outside. Are you chicken?" he asked.

I said, "Yes, I'm chicken."

Then someone told him I knew *karate* and he said, "I hear you're a *kung-fu* turkey?"

I said, "Yes, I am."

I stood my ground and pretended that I knew *karate* and I guess he got scared, because he backed down and never bothered me again. Things like this happened. I think they got me mixed up with my friend who really knew *karate*.

That's how I dealt with Canadian people in Canada. But we noticed the Japanese Canadians who are living in Canada are different from people who come from Japan, even though we all look the same. I can see *Nisei* people (second generation) and *Issei* (first generation immigrants) are pretty much the same. But *Sansei* and *Yonsei* (third and fourth generation) people who were born here look Japanese, but they are not Japanese on the inside. Sometimes they say, "I am Japanese." Sometimes they say, "I'm not Japanese, I'm Canadian." That is really interesting to hear. Also, how often do you see Japanese Canadian people get married to each other? Not often. If there are ten couples, then maybe two couples are both Japanese Canadians. For people who are born here and go to school here, to them they do not feel different from other Canadians. To us, coming from outside, this seems very strange. But then, even my own kids act more like Canadians than Japanese people.

I went back to Japan at the end of 1973. I saved money and I said, "That's it." I had been here for two and a half years. I said, "I'm not going to come back. This country's not for me." So I went home and I stayed there for five months, then I said, "This is not the same Okinawa where I grew up because everything is so small, after I spent two and a half years in Canada. There's so much open space there." So I said, "Maybe I should go back and see." It wasn't because I hated Japan or anything. When I got back here, I started working in the meat plant again. So then I was working and working, but when I had a good day, I would say, "Yeah, I'm going to stay another day." But if I had a tough day, I'd say, "I'm going to go home tomorrow." I kept going like this for about three years. That's when I started working at a big grocery store.

That was a very big change for me, because I thought maybe I could only work at that meat plant. I never thought I would be able to work at a big store like that. Of course, I couldn't speak very good English and I didn't know how to cut roasts and steaks, but they hired me. How it happened was that one of the guys that I knew from the meat plant had left his job to go and be the assistant meat manager at this big store. So he asked me if I wanted to work at his store. He talked to his store manager and meat manager for me, and for one month, I went every day, sometimes twice a day, because the store manager said he was going to let me know whether he was going to hire me or not. Every time I went there, I said, "Good afternoon, did you find out today?" He said, "No," and I said, "Thank you very much," and I went away.

Finally the store manager said, "He's here again? I'd better hire him, otherwise he's going to come and see me again every day."

I had just started working in the meat department of the store, and one day a lady and her son came to buy fish. She was an older Japanese lady, just like my grandmother. Her youngest son still lived with her. She talked to me in Japanese. She asked me about salmon. Japanese people know the best part of salmon is the part just behind the head. Canadian people throw away this part because it doesn't look nice, like salmon steak. But Japanese people like to eat it because it tastes good. So she asked me to save all these parts for her. She asked me if I came from Japan. When I said, "Yes," she started asking me many questions, so I told her I came here by myself and my family was all in Okinawa.

"Oh," she said, "It's so hard. Come to my house for supper." So I went to her house. Some days I was there for breakfast, lunch and supper. On my days off, I used to pick up her friends. All these old ladies would start cooking *manju* or *mochi* (Japanese desserts), and I would sit and listen to them talk, and I would have lunch and supper and then I would give them rides home.

So, to me, if I hadn't met that lady I don't know what would have happened. I call her *bachan* (grandma) because she's just like a grandma to me. The Okinawan Cultural Society was very good, but this lady did more for me, more than anybody. She is not Okinawan, but she came from Japan as a picture bride when she was only eighteen years old to get married to a farmer in Raymond. When her husband died, she moved into Lethbridge to live with her son. She knows how hard it can be to live in Canada and not be able to speak English. She acted just like my grandma. She "gave me heck" when I didn't do well. She showed me things and taught me. Then I said to myself, "My goodness, I have to be like her. I have to try my best to help some other people. I just can't complain about it." I learned so much from her.

So in 1977, I said to myself, "If I want to go back to Japan, I have to do it now. I can't wait until I get old. What should I do, stay here, or go back?" So I thought about it. I spent time and I thought about this, what I needed if I stayed here and if I was going to go back, what I would do there. Then I decided to stay here. I thought about so many things, because I knew my parents were going to get old and maybe I wouldn't be able to be with them, and I said, "Is that OK, or is it not?" Then I said, "OK, I'm going to stay here. So that means I have to push myself." So I became a Canadian citizen in 1977. After that, I never thought, "I'm going to go back to Japan," anymore. Then I tried my best all the time, as much as I could do. I attended all those Okinawan Cultural Society activities and of course, I had to spend lots of time with *bachan*.

When I decided to settle down and raise a family, I went back to Japan for my wife. Most young men who came over on the program didn't marry Canadian girls. Most of them went back to Japan to find a wife. Before, I had friends who all went to the same high school. One of my friends had a sister who was my friend too. She had grown up in a farming village on a small island in Okinawa, but had left home at age fifteen to go to high school on mainland Okinawa because they didn't have a high school on her island.

In Japan, boyfriends and girlfriends in high school never even hold hands. I went home in January 1979 and I went to visit her and asked her to marry me and come to Canada. I already had a house, but I didn't tell her what it was like in Canada. I brought her a box of potato chips. She had never seen them before. She had never thought about Canada before. She grew up on a small island in Okinawa, so it was hard for her to understand how big Canada was.

We got married in Japan in July and she came here in August. Because I had Canadian citizenship, we had to get married again in Canada, so we had a second wedding in September. She had a beautiful silk *kimono* in bright colours. It was not like the white wedding dresses they wore here. We had a honeymoon in Hawaii.

My wife had never been outside Japan before. She was so used to sleeping on the floor on a *futon* in Japan, that she didn't understand the Western style bed in the hotel. One day she was so surprised at how the chambermaid was making the bed and taking off the sheets. We had been sleeping on top of the sheets.

The worst part, though, was getting used to the cold weather. Where we are from in Okinawa, the coldest it would get is ten degrees Centigrade. We thought that was very cold, I guess because it was very humid. My wife had never seen snow and she couldn't believe how cold it could get here. When I first came, in cold winter weather, I could hardly breathe when I was outside and my whole body would be aching and sore. But we got used to it.

We had three children, two boys and one girl. We miss our families in Okinawa and our kids say, "Why don't we have any cousins, like other kids do?" So we spend a lot of time with the people in the Southern Alberta New Japanese Immigrant Society. They have a lot of social events, like picnics and parties, and we know all the other families. It helped my wife, especially, because she could talk to the other wives who came here from Japan too. We're not the same, like other Japanese Canadians who have been working here for a long time. They had their own organization, the Lethbridge and District Japanese Canadian Association, which was set up before we got to Canada. But for some reason, the two groups never got together till much later.

A few years later, at my grocery store, they said they would give a buy-out to people who had been working there for a long time. I decided that this was a good chance to go back to farming. I would never have been able to save up so much money to make a down payment on a farm and I didn't want to work for someone else. A lot of my friends were still working for other farmers. After twenty or twenty-five years, they knew all about the watering, fertilizing and harvesting schedules, and worked themselves up to be foremen, but they didn't own any land or machinery.

Back in those days, there was a pretty good market even for small farmers to make a good living by growing potatoes and selling them to factories in southern Alberta, to make French fries and potato chips. I started off with just one tractor, on a quarter section of land. The boys were still young and so my wife had to help me with the farm work. She even helped out by picking rocks in the fields. Farmers always have to do that. The rocks seem to come out of nowhere and we had to pick them up so they wouldn't get in the way of the plough. I had to call her out to help me hitch up or unhook the plough from the tractor. We would do just half the field at a time, not like nowadays when we have a tractor for each part of the process: ploughing, seeding, and harvesting.

When the kids got older, they started to help me on the farm. My operation started getting bigger, especially because there were more trade deals for shipping potatoes. When York Farms was working on a deal with Japan, they sent over some Japanese businessmen and they liked it because there were a lot of Japanese Canadian potato farmers. York Farms started shipping potato products to Japan, Hong Kong, and China. After that, we could buy more land and equipment. Over the years, we went from one hundred to eight hundred acres of land. It's a year-round operation and takes a lot of work. We fill all the buildings in the fall and in the wintertime we haul the potatoes to the different factories close by.

Both our sons helped a lot. When they were in high school, they helped on weekends and in the summer. Even when they were going to university, they came back to work on the farm. I think they are like me. They like farming. I hope they are going to take over the whole business someday.

I am thankful for every day. My life has been so happy. I paid ten dollars for Canadian citizenship, the best investment I ever made! The exchange program was good too, to help people understand each other more. Now I help young people from Okinawa come here for exchange visits, to learn more about Canada. All Japanese people who come here love Canada. I want people from Canada to go to Okinawa too. My own kids visited Okinawa many times, but they don't want to live there. They can register as Japanese citizens until age eighteen, but they don't want to. You have to leave Canada to understand Canada.

Now my home is here and we are proud to be Japanese and Canadian. But it doesn't matter if we are Canadian, we are still Japanese. We should understand the Japanese culture. We should learn the culture and history of both Japan and Canada, the good and bad sides of both.

10

REDRESS

Saburo Morita

I am *Nisei*, born on Vancouver Island. We had a pretty good life there before the war. My dad worked for Mr. Imayoshi of the Fanny Bay Logging Company for over ten years. One day, he decided to strike out on his own and started a shingle mill in Courtenay, B.C. After running this mill for a few years, he got together with a fellow who had ties with a Japanese company that needed logs in Japan. So with the Mitsubishi Company in Vancouver, he decided to invest money and buy timber from Vancouver Island and ship logs to Japan. As we came of age, my brothers and I would help him with the business. We were a pretty successful operation until the evacuation came along, and then suddenly, it was all over.

Because our company was connected directly with Japan, we were first on the list for having our property seized. Everything was confiscated. The Mitsubishi Company had put a lot of money away for my dad's retirement, but because it was a Japanese company, he lost all that money and never got any compensation. He lost thousands of dollars that had accumulated in his pension fund.

At the time I was twenty-three years old, so I understood everything that was going on. When the war started, the government seized everything and shut down our camp. They even had a custodian living right in the camp to keep an eye on everything so that we couldn't dispose of logging equipment, all our trucks, or whatever. We didn't feel any fear for ourselves. Even the soldiers felt really bad that they had to come in with bayonets on the ends of their rifles, just to take the phone off the wall. It was unreal, but those were the things that happened. We just accepted it. We felt that if this was the way the government wanted to do things, they had to do it.

Our family was one of the first to go into Hastings Park, because Vancouver Island was evacuated first. They came and said, "In so many hours, you have to pack up." The maximum luggage weight was a hundred fifty pounds per person. Suddenly, we had no jobs and we had no income. So being young, I thought, "Well, I may as well go out and get a job," so I went to Woodfibre, to the pulp and paper mill and worked there with a couple of other guys. It was up the Sunshine Coast towards Powell River and Sechelt. They let us work there for a few months until they evacuated Woodfibre, and then we were all supposed to go to work camp. But since my parents were in Hastings Park, I managed to catch a cab and go there, without going with the rest of the crew to a road camp. After only a short stay, all the loggers at Hastings Park had to go to Slocan to clear the area for the government to build houses for all the evacuees. So I ended up in Popoff and Slocan in the interior of B.C.

From Slocan, eighteen of us young fellows got a job offer to go to Albreda, north of Kamloops, to a sawmill up towards Blue River. It was up on the highway toward Kamloops, around Jasper and Edmonton. But the sawmill shut down while we were working there and we didn't know where we were supposed to go, so we just caught the train and came back to Slocan without travelling permits. In those days, Japanese people had to have travelling permits from the RCMP in order to travel, but we just got on the Canadian National Railroad train back to Kamloops, then caught a bus and got back into Slocan. People had seen us on the train, but they didn't bother to notify anybody.

When we got back to Slocan, the man from the B.C. Security Commission asked us, "How did you get back, you boys?"

"We just came back."

"But where are your travelling permits from the RCMP?"

After that, we were "in the bad books" of the Security Commission, so they decided to send us to Ontario to work for the Pigeon Timber Company to cut pulpwood in Fort William, Ontario. It wasn't a prisoner-of-war camp, but they wanted to send us somewhere. We had a permit to go to work for "Pigeon Timber Company, Fort William, Ontario."

We got to Fort William and we were all ready to get off the train. But the soldiers on the platform, with bayonets on their rifles, wouldn't let us off because the Pigeon Timber Company's head office was in Fort William, but we were supposed to go to their camp, which was in Neys, another six hours train ride.

They said, "You're going to Neys."

But we said, "Our tickets read, 'Fort William.'"

"Yes, the head office is Fort William, but you're supposed to go to Neys."

When we got to Neys, we found out the train didn't stop at the station. It just slowed down because it was an uphill terrain. We had to throw our baggage off the train and jump off, and then walk back a mile to the station. But that wasn't the worst part. It was already November and it was ten or fifteen degrees below Fahrenheit and all we had were B.C. clothes: trench coats, oxfords, and no long johns. They wanted us to go to camp, twenty-one miles further from the station, by horse and sleigh. We didn't like that idea, so we had a meeting at the station at Neys and decided: "We're not staying here. Let's catch the next train back to Fort William."

When the train came through at midnight we hopped on it—without tickets. In those days the CPR had telegraph service. So the guy at Neys telegraphed the guy at Fort William and said: "Those Japanese boys are coming back to Fort William."

When we got back to Fort William, the soldiers with bayonets were there again, and they said, "Go back to camp!"

They gave us two choices: either go back to camp and go to work, or go to Petawawa to a prisoner-of-war camp. We knew we didn't want to go to any POW camp and wear those uniforms with the big red dots on our backs for targets. We had a meeting and said, "OK, let's go back and work in the camp, even though it's so cold and out in the middle of the wilderness." It was terribly cold and we had to take turns running behind the sleigh. We had to keep moving to keep warm, or we would freeze. It was hard, but we just said, "This is the way it is."

Many things happened to a lot of people, but it was the older folks who really lost the most. When it came to the Redress, we *Niseis* just felt that maybe the government should compensate the seniors, who had worked all their lives and lost their life possessions. It was not so much for the young people. Before he died, my dad knew the Redress movement was going on because I was involved in going to all these meetings. He thought it was a good thing, but he didn't ever get any compensation because he passed away before it was all finalized. He didn't have any plans for the money because he was too old. He never thought about what he would do with it.

Mostly the people on the Redress Committee were *Niseis.* I think the *Sanseis* felt that they really didn't want to get too involved to press the government for any injustices. Maybe they thought that "stepping into the spotlight" could harm them more than what we were trying to achieve. Most *Sansei* people weren't really old enough to understand what had been involved with the evacuation. It was mostly *Nisei* people who went through all the inconveniences of the evacuation, but they didn't talk about it much.

The Redress movement was part of a larger human rights issue. The young lawyers who were on the Redress Committee did a lot of work, more than we did. I don't know whether the government paid them or not. But they put in a lot of time. A lot of them were young female lawyers who had families. So they sacrificed a lot too. There were about fifty to sixty people on the national committee. We worked for three to five years, attending about fifty to seventy-five meetings, all told. There were a lot of politics involved, but we did our best for what we thought was right.

A lot of people worked hard on the Redress effort, and they needed the whole support of the Japanese Canadian people. On the Redress Committee, there were representatives from all across Canada. The people in Manitoba were the most aggressive and if it weren't for the leader of that group, I don't think the Redress movement would have gone as far or achieved as much. There were some very knowledgeable people on the Redress Committee. The people who were involved with the Redress had a conviction that we were going to do our utmost to achieve it for the Japanese people. It was not for our own gain, but for the Japanese people as a whole, who were entitled to Redress.

Our role as the southern Alberta representatives was to bring back the information from the committee meetings for input from the people of southern Alberta. We would have meetings here, with about eight people attending, and mostly we went along with the decisions of the larger committee.

The everyday work on the committee was sometimes tough. Two of us volunteered to do most of the travelling to meetings, because our job schedules allowed us flexible hours. But we had personal lives and family commitments too. There were two of us from southern Alberta who did most of the travelling to all the meetings and although we got reimbursed for our travel expenses, there were a lot of miscellaneous things that came up.

When the meetings were called, we just automatically went. At times, even we got discouraged and thought, "We're putting in a lot of time, but are we really going to achieve whatever we are trying to, our final goal of Redress?" The meetings were always in Winnipeg or Vancouver or Toronto, lasting three to five days. We tried to cut the expenses down and often drove instead of taking the plane.

One time, we got a call to go to Winnipeg in November. Even though it was blizzarding, we drove the fourteen hours to Winnipeg. We had to stay in Swift Current the night before because we couldn't go any further. The next meeting was called in Vancouver in the middle of winter, and it was snowing, so we couldn't make it over the Coquihalla Pass because it was closed. So we had to go to Kamloops, around the south route to Merritt, and to Vancouver. But we had to go through another snowstorm to finally get there.

Some members on the local Redress Committee were worried about a possible negative reaction from the general public. What would people say to an announcement that Japanese people would receive a lump sum of money as financial compensation for their losses in the evacuation? In order to decrease any backlash, we thought maybe we should donate back to the community.

We ended up donating an amount that was matched by the federal government, to provide all the electric beds on the fourth floor of the new Regional Hospital in Lethbridge. There's a plaque at the entrance of the fourth floor that acknowledges this contribution from the Lethbridge and District Japanese Canadian Association. Funding was also provided for a laparoscope to St. Michael's Hospital, as well as five thousand dollars to a trust fund for each of the hospitals in the surrounding areas of Taber, Magrath, Picture Butte, and Raymond. The local members of Coaldale chose to do their own fund drive and provided a Handibus for their community. Then the University of Lethbridge and the Lethbridge Community College were each given an Endowment Fund that provides annual scholarships to any student who meets certain requirements at the post-secondary level of education.

I don't think there was much backlash from the community. I never got any. I think the rest of the people of southern Alberta had come to accept the Japanese people, because over the years they had fit in so well in their communities. They never caused any trouble with the law and by their determined attitude of trying to succeed, I think that the Japanese people built up respect for themselves.

We had very little comment from the general public. Ninety percent were unaware of what had happened to the Japanese people and their assets. For instance, my uncle who was about thirty at the time of the evacuation, had a brand new Ford convertible. In those days, you had to turn all the cars in to the government. So when they came to round up all the cars, one police officer said, "It's a shame to turn this car in. I'll buy it."

My uncle said, "OK, I'll sell it to you." He let him take the car, but he never saw that person again. He never saw the car. He never saw the money. It was a brand new Ford convertible. He would have lost it anyway, but just the idea that people took advantage and just helped themselves. That's only one case. How many others were in the same situation? How many other things happened across Canada, stories that never came out, where people never said a word? It's amazing what really went on.

A few years ago, my brother-in-law met a guy in Phoenix. He was a retired Canadian army veteran. After the war, the government gave him a strawberry farm in Surrey. Now he's retired, sold his land and he's a millionaire. He knows what happened to the Japanese people, that their property was taken away and given to returning vets, and feels kind of bad about what happened.

I think the Redress movement was a good thing, but I don't think that Japanese people really felt any different afterward. In most cases, it was really too late. A lot of people were dead and gone. Most of the rest of them had come to terms with how things had turned out, didn't expect anything, and didn't want to "rock the boat."

My father wasn't resentful or bitter, even though he had everything taken away when he was looking toward retirement. I think Buddhist teachings helped him, saying that today and what you do today, is the most important. We don't know what's going to happen in the future and tomorrow isn't here yet. Yesterday is gone, so what you do today is what really matters.

BIBLIOGRAPHY

Adachi, Ken. *The Enemy that Never Was: A History of the Japanese Canadians.* Toronto: McClelland & Stewart, 1976.

Bock, Vera, illus. *A Child's Book of Poems.* New York: The Peter Pauper Press, no date.

Broadfoot, Barry. *Years of Sorrow, Years of Shame: The Story of the Japanese Canadians in World War II.* Toronto: Doubleday Canada, 1977.

Makabe, Tomoko. *Picture Brides: Japanese Women in Canada.* Multicultural History Society of Ontario, 1995.

Morgan, Grace, and C.B. Routley, ed. *Poems for Boys and Girls, Book Two.* Toronto: Copp Clark Co., 1965.

Nakayama, Gordon G. *Issei: Stories of Japanese Canadian Pioneers.* Toronto: NC Press, 1984.

Nishiki, Nikkei Tapestry: A History of Southern Alberta Japanese Canadians. Lethbridge, AB: Lethbridge and District Japanese Canadian Association, 2001.

Kogawa, Joy. *Obasan.* Markham, ON: Penguin Books Canada, 1981.

Young, C.H., and H.R.Y. Reid. *The Japanese Canadians.* Toronto: The University of Toronto Press, 1938.

PHOTOGRAPHS

This collection of photos is not meant to represent the specific characters in the book. Most of the photos have been obtained from the Sir Alexander Galt Museum and Archives, Lethbridge, AB.

Other photos have been submitted by: Taka Kinjo, Reyko Nishiyama, Frank Sato, and Marjory Tomomitsu.

Henry Kojun Iwaasa, age 14-16 years old. Speculated to have been taken during the 31st year of the Meiji Reign and at the time of his departure from Kobe, Japan. He disembarked in Victoria, British Columbia on 14 April 1898, from the ship "Empress China." In the early 1900's he travelled from California to Utah, working on railroads, farms and in sugar beet fields. He adopted Canadian citizenship and became a farmer and landowner at Raymond.

Raymond & District Buddhist Temple at Raymond, Alberta. The temple was built in 1903 and was originally a school that was later converted for use as the Mormon Church. The Buddhist community of Raymond purchased the building in 1929 for $5,000.

Mr. Yoichi (Harry) Hironaka dressed in a three piece suit and tie. Photograph was taken to send to his picture bride, Tsuki Kanehiro, in Japan. Yoichi was born in 1884 in Japan and came to Canada in 1907. The marriage was arranged by their families. They exchanged photos, met for the first time April 9, 1913 in Vancouver, and were married the next day.

Tsuki and Akira Hironaka in Japan (about 1920) visiting her relatives. Mrs. Hironaka is on the lower right side holding son Akira (Ikey).

Yoshihika (Joe) Miyanaga while at a logging camp near Mission City, British Columbia. (1924)

Kazuo James Sato in front of a beet shack at Taber, Alberta. A bathhouse is in the background, and the cistern is beside the shack on the left. (1945)

The Young Buddhist Association baseball team at Raymond, Alberta. (1935).

Students, Grades 1-9, at the Mammoth School near Raymond, Alberta. Front row, left to right: Hisashi Matsuno, Yutaka Matsuno, Alvin Court, Yoshiyuki Oishi. Second row, left to right: Mae Koyata, Reyko Karaki, Sumiko Iwaasa, Barbara Turner, Chizuko Matsuno, Yuriko Saka, Fusako Takeda. Third row, left to right: Takeshi Koyata, Jeaunne Iwaasa. Fourth row, left to right: Myrtle Court, Fumiko Koyata, Kuniko Iwaasa, Raymond Court, Natsuko Koyata. Back row, left to right: Kenichi Hatanaka (partly hidden), Wallace Court, Yasuko Iwaasa, Keith Turner. (1935).

Members of the Buddhist Church in Raymond gathered together in celebration of the 10th Anniversary of the church. Reverend Kawamura is sitting to the left of a visiting Reverend who is dressed in the full ministerial gown. (1939).

Harry Higa in uniform. He was a Sergeant in the Canadian Army Service Corps. He joined the Army in 1940, went overseas in 1941, and served in France, Belgium and Holland until the end of the war.

Japanese men, women and children with their personal belongings, waiting to load onto a farm truck at Picture Butte, Alberta. Photo was taken when Japanese evacuees arrived at the Picture Butte Canadian Pacific Railway station from Mission, British Columbia in April 1942.

Sato family home in the Kennedy district of Surrey, British Columbia. Left to right: Kazuo James, Chiye Sherry, Teruko Anne, Yoshio Frank, Akisaburo, Moto. (1930).

Eugene and Susan Hattori. Eugene was the first child born in Lethbridge of Japanese evacuee parents.

Haruichi Tomomitsu standing in front of a sugar beet loader on the Joe Milder farm near Barnwell, Alberta. (1949).

Brothers Don and Lloyd Yamagishi standing in front of their family car, a 1950 Pontiac, on the Harris farm near Taber, Alberta. (1951).

Some members of the Yamagishi family in front of their first home in Lethbridge, Alberta. Back row (L-R) Shizue (mother), Irene and Marjory. Front row (L-R) Rick and Lloyd. (1953).

Bridal party of Misae Hironaka. Flo Senda (sister of Misae) was the matron of honour and is standing to the left. Two other bridesmaids are at the right. The two flower girls in the front are Gaye Hironaka (niece of the bride) and Mae Senda (Flo's daughter). Misae Hironaka married Akira Masuda in a Buddhist ceremony. (1954).

Twenty-year reunion at Lethbridge, AB. of some of the "new immigrants" from Japan who came to Canada to work on sugar beet farms in southern Alberta. Front row (L-R): Jocky Obaka, Yuki Nagoya, Junji Kuno, Jerry Nagai, Tosh iharu Ochikawa, Shane Nishi. Back row (L-R): Kazuhiko Kanno, Jerry Kinjo, Miekey Noji, Taka Kinjo, Takao Hirose, Peter Kinjo, Sachi Nagahama, Kenny Nakatani, Fumio Yokata. (April 1971).

ISBN 1-41205935-6

9 781412 059350

Edwards Brothers Malloy
Thorofare, NJ USA
June 22, 2015